IMAGES
of America

EARLY SPOKANE

This illustration shows the Washington Territory of Spokan Falls. (TASBC.)

IMAGES
of America

EARLY SPOKANE

Don Popejoy and Penny Hutten

ARCADIA
PUBLISHING

Published by Arcadia Publishing
Charleston, South Carolina

Library of Congress Control Number: 2010926989

For all general information, please contact Arcadia Publishing:
Telephone 843-853-2070
Fax 843-853-0044
E-mail sales@arcadiapublishing.com
For customer service and orders:
Toll-Free 1-888-313-2665

Visit us on the Internet at www.arcadiapublishing.com

*Dedicated to the students in Don's history classes and
Penny's grandchildren, Hunter, Brandon, and Katelyn—
may they all enjoy the adventure of Early Spokane*

CONTENTS

ACKNOWLEDGMENTS

Our greatest debt is to Tony and Suzanne Bamonte for generously sharing their time, knowledge, and pictures. Thanks to the Inland Empire Railway Historical Society and, in particular, Gene Hawk, Ted Halloway, Michael Denuty, and Wayne Shaw. Special thanks to Reva Dean, Northwest librarian; Jane Davey, Museum of Arts and Culture archivist; Loyce Lewis; Laura Arksey; Stephanie Plowman, Gonzaga University archivist; Janet Hauck, Whitworth University archivist; Jim Kershner, *Spokesman-Review*; Carlton Oaks, chief executive officer of the Spokane Masonic Temple; Sue Walker, secretary/treasurer of the Spokane Police Museum; Sister Pam White of Sisters of Providence; Ron Oscarson; Jean Adams; Rob Goff; Linda Crump; Mary McKee; Larry Pointer; Duane Broyles; Bob Seagel; Peter Coffin; Richard Hazelmyer; Bob Clouse; Gary Nance; Dorothy and Daryll Bahr; Frank Peltier; Al Hughes; Loren Meierding; Gail Kersey; Evelyn Varga; Dean Ladd; Don Dashiell; Barbara Cochran; Wendy Cowden; Linda Willard; Jay Moyer; Sarah Higginbotham; Devon Weston, and Donna Libert from Arcadia Publishing.

These books were a bedrock of information during the writing of *Early Spokane*: Mrs. Downing Bailey's *Why Did I Sell Spokane Falls?*; Rev. Jonathan Edwards's book *History of Spokane County 1900* and the use of his phrase "Brave Men and Devoted Women"; Nelson Durham's *History of the City of Spokane 1912 Volumes I–III*; *The Inland Empire Volumes I–IV* by George W. Fuller (1928); *News for an Empire* by Ralph E. Dyar; *Spokane Corona Eras and Empires* by Edmund T. Becher; *Shaping Spokane* by John Fahey; The Pacific Northwestern publications Volumes 1-53; Tornado Creek Publications; *Spokane and the Inland Northwest* by Tony and Suzanne Bamonte, *The Spokane Aviation Story* and *The McGoldrick Lumber Company Story* by Jim McGoldrick, *Manito Park* by Tony and Suzanne Bamonte, *Life Behind the Badge*, *Miss Spokane* by Tony and Suzanne Bamonte, *Spokane Set in Stone* by Dick Jensen; *The White Cascade* by Gary Krist; *Bold Spirit* by Linda Lawrence Hunt, *Exploring Spokane's Past* by Barbara Cochran (1984), *First Class for 100 Years 1889–1989: Spokane Public Schools*; and finally, the digital media using historylink.org and Google's online archived newspapers.

The images in this volume appear courtesy of the Northwest Room, Spokane Public Library (NRSPL); the following collections of the Northwest Room, Spokane Public Library: Teakle (TCNRSPL), E. T. Becher (ETBCNRSPL), and Boughton (BCNRSPL); the Jerry Quinn Collection of photographs by Charles Libby (JQCPBCL); the Tony and Suzanne Bamonte Collection (TASBC); the Richard Sheuerman Collection (RSC); and the Don Popejoy Collection (DPC).

INTRODUCTION

In the heart of the Columbia Plateau lies Spokane, a vast and varied landscape that was sculpted millions of years ago by extraordinary basalt eruptions and floods from the Miocene era, followed by the enormous floods from the receding Ice Age glaciers about 12,500 years ago. Spokane is truly the heart of Eastern Washington, a virtual Inland Empire, surrounded by formidable mountain ranges, which comprise the Rocky Mountains to the east, the Selkirks to the north, the Wenatchee Mountains (an extension of the Cascade Mountains), and the Columbia River to the west. The Snake River to the south cuts through the fertile Palouse Country (considered to be the breadbasket of the Columbia Plateau), and various regions around the world. Beyond the Snake River rise the Blue Mountains, also referred to as "the Blues" by the Oregon Trail pioneers who ventured from the Missouri River area westward, responding to the call of Manifest Destiny.

This enormous arena would be the last frontier in North America to be settled by white Europeans. This "Oregon Territory" would bring, over a period of decades, thousands of new settlers. Among the first would be the fur traders, followed by the missionaries, prospectors, miners, soldiers, farmers, merchants, and finally the surveyors and the railroads. However, this wild and romantic landscape had been the home of the First Peoples for thousands of years: people of the Spokan, Coeur d'Alene, Yakama, Palouse, Walla Walla, Nez Perce, and other Indian nations.

The first white men to see and explore this vast and untamed wilderness were the Spanish, English, Russian, and Americans who were searching for "brown gold" (beaver pelts) up and down the Pacific coast, which would bring them untold wealth in China. The first white men to write about the Spokane River were Lewis and Clark in 1805, on their way to the Pacific Ocean. Arriving at today's Almota, Washington, via the Snake River on October 11, 1805, the two captains referred to the Skeet-ko-mish Indians (Spokan) who live at the falls of a large river, about 125 miles to the north.

The first non-Indian to visit the Spokane River was Finnan MacDonald, employed by David Thompson of the Hudson Bay Company. David Thompson, also known as "the Star Man," came to the Spokane Country to trap beaver and establish his presence along the Columbia River from Canada to the Pacific Ocean. In 1810, Finnan MacDonald and Jaques (Jacko) Finlay were sent by Thompson to the confluence of the Pointed Heart River (Spokane) and the Spokane River (Little Spokane) to set up a trading post, which would be established as Spokane House. David Thompson arrived in 1811 and enjoyed a total monopoly with the Spokanes until John Jacob Astor's company arrived in 1812 to establish his trading post, Fort Spokane. Note that trading posts were called forts, even though there was no military presence there.

The Spokan welcomed the traders and were pleased to have the North West Company fort located at one of their main villages. This relationship gave them the advantage of obtaining guns, ammunition, and other trade items. They were the envy of other tribes and became the wealthy middlemen on the Spokane River. Others would follow, equally leaving their mark on the Inland Northwest. Men such as David Douglas, the first naturalist in the area; Alexander Ross, fur trader

7

and noted historian; Nathaniel Wyeth, a Boston trader, and entrepreneur; Capt. B. L. E. Bonneville, a Hudson's Bay Company man, a U.S. Army explorer and adventurer; Peter Skene Ogden, a fur trade brigade leader in the Snake River country and a man of influence along the middle and lower Columbia River; and the Reverend Samuel Parker, instrumental in bringing missionaries to the Pacific Northwest, as well as the "black book" to the indigenous Indian people.

They have been here for thousands of years, these "Children of the Sun." Just like the Spokane River, their hearts flowed with the vibrant sounds of life. The river provided rich and healthy staples—along with the cold, pure water comes the salmon, the deer, wild berries, camas, wapato, and all the essentials that would make this region a veritable Garden of Eden.

As the Inland Northwest became over run by strangers, one man stepped forward to try to save his people from annihilation. As a young boy, Spokan Garry was sent by the Hudson's Bay Company to the Red River Missionary School in Winnipeg, Canada, to learn of the white man's way and his religion. Spokan Garry would come back home in 1831 at the age of 20, and start the first school in the Northwest where he taught the Indian people basic agriculture, reading, writing, and the Christian religion. His school closed in 1840, whereupon Spokan Garry spent his time among his people, the Middle Spokans, teaching them the ways to survive the white man's onslaught. Over the winter of 1870–1871, Garry held a religious revival among his people and opened a second school. Garry would die in 1892, a broken man caught between two cultures.

White settlement flooded the region, first by the American Board of Commissioners for foreign missions, represented by the Cushing and Eells families who settled in with the Spokan Indians, the Reverend H. T. Cowley in the Spokan Falls, the Spalding family in Nez Perce country, and the Whitman family in Cayuse land. In a very short span of time, settlements appeared across this vast and varied landscape, and in the heart of the Palouse Country, Spokane Bridge, followed by the Spokan Falls, were established.

The urge to fulfill the credo of Manifest Destiny, the pre–Civil War land rushes, the discovery of gold in Montana, Idaho, and Washington, the fertile land of the Willamette Valley, and the vast amount of government and private roads, all combined to lead people from every walk of life to the Inland Empire, truly a Garden in the center of the Columbia Plateau.

Spokane Bridge, the first permanent white settlement in the Spokane valley 18 miles east of the future site of Spokan Falls, was one of two bridges to cross the Spokane River until 1881. Spokane Bridge was built in 1864 near the major campsite of the Coeur d'Alene Indians and the little community consisted of a store, a hotel (which had a dining room), and the first post office in Spokane County. Michael M. Cowley bought the bridge in 1872 and built his home, as well as a trading post, on the north side of the river. The house still stands and the post office was active until 1958.

James Nettle Glover and Jasper Matheney arrived at the falls in 1873 from Oregon. Glover, later known as the "Father of Spokane," had a vision for the potential of the falls. Instinctively, Glover knew that by utilizing the powerful water from the falls, he could establish mills that would be capable of providing for a large town. He was so impressed with the area, he named it Spokan Falls, after both the Spokan Indians and the falls. He bought a working muley sawmill from the first settlers, James J. Downing and Seth R. Scranton, plus 160 acres, which is now the downtown area of Spokane. He built the first store with a post office and persuaded Frederick Post to open a gristmill at the falls by giving him forty acres of land. As the town started growing, some of the earliest inhabits were Rev. H. W. Cowley, Rev. Samuel Havermale, banker Anthony Cannon, attorney John J. Brown, and a number of other enterprising men.

In 1879, one such man was Francis Cook. He started the area's first newspaper, *The Spokan Times*. It was a rather controversial newspaper, which upset the founding fathers. One story described Anthony Cannon and his son-in-law, Bascomb Bennett, showing up at Cook's office, brandishing a revolver, and demanding a newspaper retraction. The article claimed Francis Cook struck Bennett over the head with an iron bar, kicking him down the stairs.

The catalyst to Spokane's growth was the arrival of the Northern Pacific Railroad on June 25, 1881. On July 2, 1864, the government passed the Pacific Railroad Act, spurring the Northern

Pacific and Union Pacific to build transcontinental railroads. The Northern Pacific laid tracks from Missouri to the Pacific Coast, driving the last spike in September 8, 1883. Other railroads soon would follow. On August 14, 1892, the Great Northern Railway came to Spokane on its way to the Pacific Coast. Mining in Idaho, lumber, wheat fields, and farmland in Spokane fueled the need for spur railroad lines, making Spokane the hub of the Inland Empire. Spokane became one of the most important rail centers of the United States. In 1888, Spokane had its first horse-powered streetcar, constructed and supervised by A. J. Ross. A few months later, Francis Cook built the first steam-powered streetcar, called Spokane and Montrose. Other electric lines followed, until every area of Spokane had access to streetcars. The invention of the motorcars eventually caused the streetcars to go out of business.

The Great Spokane Fire of 1889 destroyed most of the downtown area, but because of the town's immense commerce, it resurged quickly, with tents being brought in from Fort Spokane and Fort Sherman. The *Spokane Daily Chronicle* newspaper was on the street the next day, working from a tent. Entrepreneurs saw the fire as a way to start new and better businesses.

On December 2, 1890, an advertisement in the *New York Times* promoted "The Wonders of Washington," in an attempt to persuade easterners to move to the Inland Empire. In the same advertisement, A. M. Cannon used the term "the four seasons" in reference to the weather of Spokane. By 1891, the town was growing exponentially with banks, schools, colleges, hospitals, and parks as its name changed from Spokane Falls to Spokane. Many of Spokane's early entrepreneurs became millionaires.

Spokane featured a park in every area of the city, attributable to Aubrey White's idea to have John Olmsted create a park system plan in 1907. Olmsted wanted railroad tracks taken out of what eventually became Riverfront Park. This finally happened when the area was redesigned for the 1974 World's Fair. Today, Spokane is known for its Museum of Arts and Culture, outstanding hospitals, universities, colleges, schools, and as a fertile place for business. Spokane is truly a dynamic, expanding city that can nurture the future.

The Indian Congress of October 1925 was held in Spokane to attract people to the beautiful and magical Pacific Northwest. This three-day festival featured parades, lectures, a baby contest, the crowning of an "American princess," and a football game between the Jesuit school at Gonzaga and Haskell Institute, an Indian college in Kansas. As shown in the photograph above, The Indians pitched their tipis on land where their ancestors had camped for centuries. Note the smoke rising from the tipis and all the Model Ts parked near the Indian lodgings. The Spokane River runs to the north of the campsite.

One

CHILDREN OF THE SUN

As the town of Spokan Falls developed and expanded, the Spokans relocated to the confluence of Latah Creek and the Spokane River. The Spokans raised their tipis in Indian Canyon and Peaceful Valley. This c. 1880 photograph shows their campsite in Peaceful Valley, along the Spokane River, west of town. Among the traditional hide tipis, there are several tule or reed mat lodges. (ETBCNRSPL.)

Born in 1811, Spokan Garry, the youngest son of Chief Illim-Spokanee, was destined to become chief of the Middle Spokans. At the tender age of 14, Garry was chosen by the Hudson's Bay Company to become a leader and teacher for his people. Garry received a white man's education and was taught his religion at the Red River Missionary School in Winnipeg, Canada. In 1831, Garry set up the first school in the Northwest, by the confluence of two rivers known as the Pointed Heart River and the Trout River. Garry taught agriculture, how to read and write, and the Christian way of life. Garry soon became a man of two different cultures. The sadness in Chief Garry's face below reflects the strain and pressure of living in a world of change. (Above, courtesy of TCNRSPL; below, courtesy of NRSPL.)

The Spokans consisted of three different villages—the Upper, Middle, and Lower—each under its own chief and counsel, but all considered one Nation. The Middle Spokans, Chief Garry's village, consisted of the land between today's community of Tum Tum and the mouth of Latah Creek, where it joins the Spokane River. The Spokans established semipermanent camps alongside these watercourses, and their main fisheries were situated at the little falls of the Spokane, the confluence of the Pointed Heart (now Spokane River) and the Trout River or the Little Spokane River as in the picture above, the mouth of Latah Creek, and the great falls of the Spokane River. The "civilized life" of Spokan Garry, pictured at right, caused him much despair. He seemed most content while he was at his school teaching his people the Christian way of life. (Courtesy of TASBC.)

Garry's anxiety soon ended his life as a public preacher, and he closed his school in 1840. However, during the winter of 1870–1871, Garry opened his second school. He returned to preaching and started a religious revival among his people, but in early 1875, Rev. H. T. Cowley opened his Indian school and all but shut down Garry's latest endeavor. Chief Garry, a broken and bitter man, died January 12, 1892, and was buried in a wooded area on the heights near his beloved Spokane River, as seen in the image at left. Below is a photograph of a gravestone erected at Garry's burial site in the late 1890s, with the notable names of Alexander Ross, an explorer of the Columbia Plateau; Isaac I. Stevens, governor of Washington Territory; and Col. George Wright, who brought the Spokan Indian war to a violent end in September 1858. (Above, courtesy of NRSPL; below, courtesy of TCNRSPL.)

When Chief Garry died, a Spokane paper, the *Review*, made the following comment: "Alas, Poor Garry! The story of his life, interwoven with that of the death of his people, might well be made a theme of poetry, to endure long after the last Spokane has vanished from the land." In 1925, the Spokane Chapter of the Daughters of the American Revolution dedicated a granite marker over his grave. Then in 1932, a city park was named in his honor in the very area where Chief Garry allowed his horses to run. Right, Garry's daughter, Nellie, stands next to the marker. The Spokane Indians remain proud of their heritage and lifestyle. In the image below, an Indian family in their ceremonial regalia poses for a picture in the 1930s, possibly at the fairgrounds. (Above, courtesy of TCNRSPL; below, courtesy of Donahue Collection NRSPL.)

The conflict between Protestant and Catholic beliefs contributed to Garry's anxiety, and he soon stopped his public preaching and closed his school in 1840. During the winter of 1870–1871, Garry started his second school that overlooked the Spokane Valley high on the basalt bluffs at Drumheller Springs. He began preaching again and started a religious revival among his people, but in early 1875 Rev. H. T. Cowley (left) built his Indian school and shut down Chief Garry. A bitter and broken man, Garry always relied on the words he wrote in the flyleaf of his Bible: "When I remember that Jesus loves me." St. Michael's Mission Church, as seen below, was built in 1866 by Fr. Joseph Cataldo on Peone Prairie. The presence of the Catholic religion added to the religious controversies. (Above, courtesy of NRSPL; below, courtesy of TASBC.)

James Slikoewoyeh, known as "Curly Jim" to the locals, was born in 1842 and died on January 19, 1917, of pneumonia at Sacred Heart Hospital in Spokane. Curly Jim watched as an early settlement produce what James Glover later christened Spokane Falls. Curly, a full-blood Upper Spokane, became one of the local favorites and knew many of the townsfolk. Curly may have fought against the whites in the Indian wars during the 1850s, but still maintained his relationships with the white community. Curly was a fixture around the Spokane Falls area at places such as Glover Field along the Spokane River, just above the Spokane Falls, where it is thought he was born. Curly's favorite place was John W. Graham's store, where he sat in his favorite chair and told stories of long ago. (Courtesy of NRSPL.)

In 1858, Antoine Plante, the first white settler in the Spokane Valley, built a ferry across the Spokane River at Myrtle Point. Since this was initially the best place to cross the river, Plante's business was very profitable, as he charged $4 per wagon, 50¢ per person, and 15¢ per animal. The spring just above Plante's cabin was the site where, in 1855, Gov. Isaac Stevens and Spokan Garry decided the fate of the Spokans from December 3 to December 6. When Joseph Lapray built his bridge in 1865, 30 miles west of Plante's ferry crossing, just a year after the settlement of Spokane Bridge by M. M. Cowely in 1864, 18 miles to the east, Plante was forced out of business. In 1872, Plante moved back to Montana, settling in the Jocko Valley, where he died in 1890. (Courtesy of NRSPL.)

Territorial governor Isaac Stevens, pictured at right, and Capt. George McClellan were assigned by the U.S. government to locate a pass through the Cascade Mountains for the Northern Pacific Railroad. In October 1853, the two camped at the forks of Coulee Creek, which soon became known as Camp Washington. To acquire land for the railroad, Stevens began a series of treaty councils in 1855 that touched off a cultural conflict, beginning with the Yakama Indian War in 1856. The U.S. Army sent Lt. John Mullan, below, to engineer a military road from Fort Walla Walla, on the Columbia River, to Fort Benton on the Missouri River. Mullan began surveying in 1858 when the outbreak of the Spokan Couer d'Alene Indian War occurred. The year 1858 would be a tumultuous year for everyone living in the Spokane region. (Courtesy of NRSPL.)

The first major battle of the Coeur d'Alene War of 1858 began when Colonel Steptoe, pictured at left, departed Fort Walla Walla on May 6, heading for the Snake River, which would then take him north to Fort Colville; however, he had to pass through prime Spokane Indian territory. Steptoe got as far as the present Turnbull National Wildlife Refuge and the Indian encampment of Sela. With the taunts and harassment of the Indians, Steptoe decided to turn back toward the Snake River. After 10 hours of fighting, confusion, and running, Steptoe's command fought their way to the present town of Rosalia, Washington, and took to the heights. On May 17, the Battle of Pine Creek, represented in the illustration below, raged until dark. The Nez Perce guide, Chief Timothy, trapped on the hill with Steptoe, brokered a deal with the Indians, and Steptoe's command escaped certain death. (Above, courtesy of NRSPL; below, courtesy of Richard Scheuerman by artist Nona Hengen.)

The Spokane Couer d'Alene Indian War came to a climatic conclusion when Col. George Wright, depicted in the drawing at right, took over command of the U.S. Army. Wright's campaign began August 7, 1858, when he left Fort Walla Walla, and camped at Granite Lake, near what is now the town of Four Lakes. Around 8:00 a.m. on September 1, Wright noted that several hundred Indians were on the heights in his front, and the Battle of Four Lakes commenced. The fight lasted six hours when the Indians finally left the battle ground, moving north to the Spokane Plains. Chief Kamaikan of the Yakima was instrumental in leading the Indians in this battle, as he had done in the Yakima War of 1856. The photograph below was taken in 1864 and shows Kamaikan wearing a feathered hairpiece and ceremonial dress with long buckskin shoulder fringes. (Above, courtesy of TCNRSPL; below, courtesy of RSC.)

Washington territorial governor Isaac Stevens, often referred to as a "young man in a hurry," held treaty councils with the Pacific Northwest Indian tribes from 1855 to 1858. Along with the Spokans were the Nez Perce, Cayuse, Umatilla, Walla Walla, Yakama, Flatheads, and many others. The first treaty council was held in May 1855 in Walla Walla, Washington Territory. Among the chiefs in attendance was Chief Aeneas of the Flatheads, as drawn below by artist Gustavus Sohon. John Webster was the Indian Agent of the Colville Reservation, just north of Spokane, from 1904 to 1914, and was considered a good representative. In the photograph above, they are, from left to right, as follows: (first row) Skolaskan, John Webster, Inspector James McLaughlin, and Aeneas (at 82 years old); (second row) Sally Nee, Robert Covington, Barnaby, Nesplem George, Miss Peterson, Thomas MacCrosson, and Orapagan. (Courtesy of NRSPL.)

By March 1887, the Lower, Middle, and Upper Spokans had moved onto their reservations, created by an act in 1881 by President Hayes. The Indian agent, a U.S. Army officer, was in charge of the management and morale of the reservations and became the mediator between the residents and the government. Above, Indian agent John Montieth is standing behind three Nez Perce men. From left to right are James Rueben, Archie Lawyer, and Mark Williams. In the photograph below are (first row, sitting) Nellie, Garry's daughter; and the small child is possibly Joseph; (second row) Billy Mason, a Spokane man; Chief Seltice of the Couer d'Alene; Chief Spokane Garry; and a nephew of Garry's; (third row, standing) Bob Flatt, interpreter; R. Gwydir, Indian agent Richard Gwydir (1887–1889); and James Gibson. (Courtesy of NRSPL.)

In 1926, The Indian Congress was again held in Spokane and featured the same festivities. This year, Jessie Jim of the Colville tribe would become the second American Princess in a ceremony held at the Davenport Hotel. In the above birds-eye view looking into Glover Field, a line of Model T's are parked or working their way down Main Street toward the stadium entrance. Numerous tipis are set-up from the various tribes around the Pacific Northwest, and the bleachers are waiting for the hundreds of spectators to show up for the day's events. The tipis were covered in standard-issue canvas, and most are void of coloring or designs, as seen below. The black smoke rising in the distance is from the Kendall Yards industrial area, and the clusters of buildings to the right are private homes. (Above, courtesy of JQCPBCL; below, courtesy of NRSPL.)

The Spokane Advertising Club was looking for a unique way to promote Spokane. Through their ad campaign they devised a "Miss Spokane" contest and the winning contestant would be named Spokane's official representative. In 1912, Marguerite Motie was chosen from among 138 hopefuls to become the first ambassador of Spokane. Due to the region's vast Native American history, the local Indian dress was adopted, and the elegant Davenport Hotel became the focal point for most of the pageants. The original Miss Spokane pageant ended in 1977, although its predecessor continues. (Courtesy of NRSPL.)

MONUMENT DEDICATION MULLAN MILITARY ROAD, GLENROSE, WASH. OCT. 28TH 1934.

As a result of Spokane's rich cultural heritage, residents in the Glenrose neighborhood dedicated a Mullan Military Road marker on October 28, 1934. Dressed in 1860's regalia, with horses and a supply wagon, the participants commemorated the days when Mullan's road came through Spokane. (Courtesy of Marilyn Moore.)

The renowned Davenport Hotel hosted the National Congress of American Indians in 1954. The congress was founded in 1944 in order to protect the rights of the American Indians. The Congress in Spokane was presided over by the great-great-grandson of Spokan Garry, Joseph R. Garry (right). Joseph was born in 1910 and attended Haskell Institute in Kansas, then transferred to Butler University in Indiana, where he studied to become a forest botanist. Joseph eventually became involved in Indian politics and won six consecutive terms as president of the Congress from 1953 to 1959. Joseph's father, Ignace Garry, was the last traditional chief of the Couer d'Alenes and enjoyed performing in native regalia at the Davenport Hotel for dignitaries visiting Spokane. In this 1954 photograph, from left to right, are the following: Isadore Garry, great-grandson of Spokan Gary and the father of Joseph K. Garry: Cleveland Kamiakin (at 84 years old); the son of Chief Kamiakin; and Joseph R. Garry holding his daughter, Priscilla, the great-great-great-granddaughter of Spokan Garry. (Courtesy of BCNRSPL.)

Cleveland Kamiakin (Piupiu K'ownot), Chief Kamiakin's youngest son, was a Yakima-Palouse leader and was active all of his life. Cleveland believed that ceremonial dances were sacred and showed "deep beauty, spiritual guidance, consolation and disciplinary power." He preserved the traditions of his people and was a respected elder. In this photograph from the 1940s, Cleveland is riding a horse at the head of a parade in Wilbur, Washington. In 1956, Cleveland was invited to the dedication of the newest dam on the Columbia River, the Chief Joseph Dam. Cleveland passed away in 1959 at the age of 89 in his home in Nesplem, and was laid to rest near where Chief Joseph was buried. (Courtesy of RSC.)

Two

THE BLACK BOOK

When Fr. Joseph Cataldo arrived in Spokane country, he asked permission to build a cabin, but since Spokan Garry was away hunting, Chief Peone could not give permission. When Garry returned, he gave his blessing and the Spokans pledged their friendship by smoking the peace pipe near a lone pine tree. Saint Michael church, built in 1866, would become a symbol and a bond between the Jesuits and the Spokans. (Courtesy of TASBC.)

At left is Fr. Peter Jean DeSmet, a Jesuit Missionary, who came to the Columbia Plateau in 1841 and set up his first missions among the Spokan, Coeur d'Alene, Colville, Flatheads, and Kalispel Indians. In August, 1845, Father DeSmet built a small log chapel near the Kettle Falls on the Upper Columbia River. Two years later, it was replaced by a hand-hewn log church, known as St. Paul's Mission. In the spring of 1859, Father DeSmet brought tribal chiefs together at a dinner to discuss peace talks after the 1858 Indian war that raged throughout the Spokane country. The talks were held at the request of Brig. Gen. William Harney. In the lower right photo, taken after dinner, are, standing left to right: (standing) Thunder Rolls, Bonaventure, DeSmet, and Mr. Francis; (seated) Victor Happy Man, Alexander, Red Feather, and Andrew Seltice. (Courtesy of NRSPL.)

The Reverend Cushing and Myra Eells, pictured at right and below respectively, along with the Reverend Elkanah and Mary Walker, established the first mission to the Spokans (Tshimakain) in 1838, near Chamokane Creek. The mission site would last until the Whitman Massacre of November 30, 1847, and then it closed its doors in March 1848. The four devoted missionaries served the Indians faithfully, leaving only after a heartbreaking plea to stay. During the nine years at the mission, the Walkers had six children, all of which Mary taught how to read and write, while the Eells raised two children of their own. After the massacre, the missionary families moved to the Willamette Valley to begin a new life. Rev. Cushing Eells and his wife returned to the area in 1859 and Cushing founded Whitman College in Walla Walla, Washington, in honor of Dr. Marcus Whitman. (Above, courtesy of TCNRSPL; below, courtesy of NRSPL.)

Fr. Joseph Cataldo, a Jesuit, built the first St. Michael's Mission church on Peone Prairie in 1866. Polatkan, a former chief of the Spokans, allowed Father Cataldo to build a small cabin. After several months, the Indians asked for a chapel, and Cataldo replaced the cabin with a new building two years later. In 1880, Father Carfagno added an Indian school, and in 1882, the mission site was moved to a different location, as seen in the photograph above. The mission church was moved one more time in 1967 to Fort George Wright in Spokane, where it could be maintained and cared for. St. Michael's Mission was in use until construction of Gonzaga was completed in 1887. In 1881, Father Cataldo, pictured at left, bought the land for the future site of Gonzaga along the banks of the Spokane River, near the majestic falls. (Above, courtesy of TASBC; below, courtesy of NRSPL.)

The oldest road through the area was also an ancient Indian trail known as the Colville-Walla Walla Road. This road accessed the Walla Walla, Snake, Palouse, and Columbia Rivers and their watersheds. The Walkers and Eells would use this route to travel from their mission site at Tshimakain to Fort Colville for supplies. The original buildings of the mission in the photograph above were built in 1908, but are now gone. The road ran right through the mission grounds and is still used to this day as State Highway 231. The Lilac tree seen below between the two structures was planted by the missionaries in 1839, the year after their arrival, and is verified by the horticulturalist department at WSU as the original. (Above, courtesy of Bob Seagle; below, courtesy of TASBC.)

This house sits near where the Tshimakain Mission house sat and was the residence of Mr. and Mrs. F. Johnson (above), sitting on the porch with their daughter, who moved onto the property just after World War One. Carl Baldwin and his family bought the property in 1936. On the mission grounds is a fresh water stream that was the source of their drinking water. The stream (left) can be seen flowing from the well house to Chamokane Creek and was being used by Merrill Baldwin and his wife in 1938. The well house still sits on the property although not in its original place, and the spring still produces cool, fresh water. Bob Seagle now lives on property that his father bought in 1948, and he recalls his friendship as a young boy with Merrill Baldwin. (Courtesy of Bob Seagle.)

After leaving the Spokane Mission in March 1848, Elkanah filed a land claim on 640 acres in Forest Grove in 1849, where he and Mary lived for the rest of their lives. Rev. Walker was the pastor of the Presbyterian Church and served as a joint pastor to the local Congregationalist Church from 1856 until 1875. Elkanah founded Pacific University in 1866 and served as a university trustee until his death in 1877. The photograph above was taken at the Walker family reunion held in October 1892. Standing in the picture, from left to right, are as follows: Joseph Elkanah, John Richardson, Cyrus Hamlin, Marcus Whitman, Abigail Korr, Levi Chamberlain, and Samuel Thompson; seated is Mary Richardson Walker, before her death in 1897. Below, in the photograph of a Methodist church picnic in Peaceful Valley during August 1884, is where Spokane Falls provided a place to play and a "Pulpit Rock" preaching platform. (Above, courtesy of Elkanah and Mary Richardson Walker Papers (Cg 57, Bx 4, F 38.12), Manuscripts, Archives, and Special Collections, Washington State University Libraries, Portrait by H. A. Crosley Studio, Forest Grove, Oregon; below, courtesy of NRSPL.)

Rev. Samuel Havermale preached the first sermon to a white congregation as the presiding elder of Methodists from north of the Snake River on November 14, 1875. Mrs. Yeaton brought an organ from Willamette Valley and played for the service. In attendance were Mr. and Mrs. Glover, and the H. T. Cowley family. The First Methodist Episcopal Church of Spokane was organized by Rev. J. H. Leard, in 1879, now known as the Central United Methodist located at 518 W. 3rd Ave. (Courtesy of JQCPBCL.)

In 1881, Fr. Joseph Cataldo converted a carpenter's shop into the Church of St. Joseph, the first Catholic Church in Spokane. Five years later, the structure was replaced by the Our Lady of Lourdes Church and a school was added, christened Sisters of the Holy Names. Finally, in 1913 the Cathedral for the Diocese of Spokane was built and called Our Lady of Lourdes Catholic Church, located on Main between Washington and Bernard. (Courtesy of JQCPBCL.)

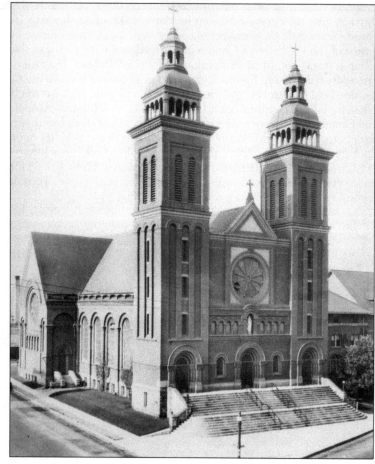

On June 10, 1883, Rev. T. G. Watson started the first Presbyterian Church of Spokane. A. M. Cannon was one of the first trustees and the Church would alternate between the Cannon building and Van Dorn Opera house for services. Francis H. Cook, the publisher of the *Spokan Times*, was one of the first elders, in 1883. The church in this picture was dedicated in 1910. (Courtesy of Mac Naughton Collection, NRSPL.)

In *African Americans in Spokane*, author Jerrelene Williamson wrote, "This photograph is of the congregation standing in front of Calvary Baptist Church in 1919. Rev. Emmett Reed, the pastor, is standing next to his wife, Pam Reed. Irene and Wallace Hagin Sr. are right in front of the church sign. Thelma (Reed) Weiseger and Wallace Hagin Jr. are two of the children in the first row." This church was founded in 1890. (Courtesy of JQCPBCL.)

Rev. William Ashley, or better known as "Billy Sunday," arrived in Spokane, January 1909 and caused a huge disturbance. People were either converting (at a record of 5,666) or they were boycotting him because of his stance on Prohibition and his teachings on temperance. The February 3, 1909 *Chronicle* headline encouraged "All Germans to boycott Billy Sunday's tented tabernacle meetings." The Soul Saving Station was an outcropping of these times. (Courtesy of JQCPBCL.)

Paramahansa Yogananda gave a series of lectures in Spokane September 1925 at the Masonic Temple, and stayed at the Davenport Hotel while on his western teaching tour. Yogananda—whose name meant bliss or divine union—lectured to sold-out auditoriums across the continent, including Carnegie Hall. Yogananda started the Self-Realization Fellowship in 1920 that emphasized unity of the world's religions and methods for attaining a personal experience with God. (Courtesy of JQCPBCL.)

Three

SILENT SENTINELS

Pres. Theodore Roosevelt visited Fort George Wright in 1911 and can be seen in this photograph, marching in step with Lt. Col. S. W. Miller. Racing alongside Roosevelt is the press corps with cameras, pencils, and notepads. Trailing the newsmen are members of the 25th Infantry, a segregated unit known as the Buffalo Soldiers. To the right is a young boy and girl, arm in arm, trying to keep up. (Courtesy of NRSPL.)

In August of 1877, George and Emma Cowen, along with seven companions, went to Yellowstone National Park. On August 24, the day of their second anniversary, they were captured, along with their companions, by the Nez Perce as they were fleeing from the U.S. Army through the nation's first National Park. Chief Joseph of the Nez Perce eventually released Emma, shown in this 1930 photograph, but George had been shot several times and was left for dead. General Howard's command rescued George, and the Cowens were reunited and returned to their hometown of Radersburg, Montana. They moved to Spokane in 1910, where George practiced law. Emma wrote about their adventures the book called *Adventures in Geyserland*, published in 1937, and gave many talks about her experiences. George died in 1926 and Emma in 1938; both are buried at Riverside Cemetery. (Courtesy of Sharon Strand.)

1810 FIRST
X SPOKANE HOUSE

FORT SPOKAN
BECAME SECOND
SPOKA E HOUSE

The first permanent white settlement west of the Rocky Mountains was established by the Northwest Company, a Canadian firm, at the confluence of the Pointed Heart (Spokane) and the Trout (Little Spokane) Rivers. The Middle Spokanes had a camp there, and the Little Spokane River had been a rich fishing site for centuries. In early 1810, David Thompson passed through the Canadian Rockies and sent Finnian McDonald and Jocko Finlay ahead to find a "profitable" location among the Spokans. McDonald and Finlay were the first white men to see the Spokane Falls (the future site of Spokane) and describe the Spokane River. Within a few months, Spokane House was flourishing as a fur trading post, when the inevitable happened: in 1811, John Jacob Astor's Pacific Fur Company set up a post a half mile away. (Courtesy of TASBC.)

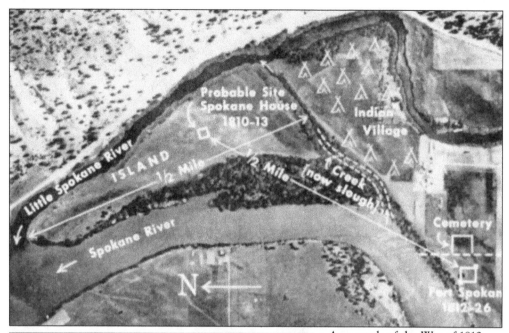

Probable Site
Spokane House
1810-13

ISLAND
½ Mile

Little Spokane River

½ Mile

Creek
(now slough)

Spokane River

Indian
Village

Cemetery

Fort Spokane
1812-26

N

As a result of the War of 1812 with Britain, the Americans gave up their post and the Canadians took over the Spokane House, positioned in the aerial view above. The Northwest Company moved all of their belongings, and Fort Spokane became Spokane House, but improved. Spokane House prospered until 1821 when the Hudson's Bay Company merged with the Northwest Company. Soon the post was considered to be in an "inconvenient" location, and in 1826 was moved to Kettle Falls on the Columbia River. Spokane House had conducted business for 16 years under three different flags: Canadian, American, and British. Jocko Finlay lived the rest of his life at the old post site. Archaeological excavations in the 1950s revealed Jocko Finlay's grave, as seen at left, complete with his clay pipe, with the initial "J" craved on it. (Courtesy of TASBC.)

After the 1858 Indian war, Lieutenant John Mullan began building the road he had surveyed several years before. Work on the military road began June 25, 1859, from Fort Walla Walla, Washington Territory. Mullan's crew worked their way over mountains, built bridges across rivers, and hacked their way through thick forests, a distance of 624 miles to Fort Benton, Montana. Mullan's Military Road was completed August 1, 1862. In 1861, Mullan stopped in the Couer d'Alene Mountains and celebrated the Fourth of July. He carved the date in a white pine tree, which stood until it was destroyed in November 1962. The photograph above dates back to 1918 and shows a marble statue of Mullan at Fourth of July Pass. In 1941, the Spokane County Pioneer Society erected a monument near a segment of the Mullan Road, as seen in the photograph below. (Courtesy of NRSPL.)

CHIEF JOSEPH

The Nez Perce War of 1877, between the non-treaty Nez Perce and the U.S. Army, led to concern for the safety of the people in the Palouse Country. Each town gathered together to protect themselves against the possibility that the Nez Perce would bring the war to their homes. The few citizens of Spokan Falls fortified themselves on an island in the Spokane River, in the home of Rev. Samuel Havermale. Although the Nez Perce never came close to any of these towns, the possibility existed and the residents took precautions. In the above photograph, the remains of Havermale's residence can be seen facing the spectacular falls, with a few homes scattered across the river to the north. Chief Joseph, pictured at left, was escorting his people to a safer place, possibly into Crow Country in Montana Territory. (Courtesy of JQCPBCL.)

Every American was affected by the Civil War that ravaged the country from 1861 until 1865, including the author's great-grandfather. Brothers William (left) and Edward Andrew Haynes, pictured at right, enlisted in Company B. 26th Infantry Volunteers on August 15, 1861. The 26th was assigned to the 1st Brigade, 4th Division, XVI Corps, Army of the Tennessee under Capt. George Reids. During Ulysses S. Grant's campaign against Vicksburg, Edward was severely wounded. William assisted the surgeon on the field in amputating his brother's right leg. William was discharged August 28, 1864, and after the war, the family moved from Rockford, Illinois, to Spokane, Washington. In the family photograph below, William with Edward are to the far right of the fron Porch (note Edward's missing right leg). Behind Edward is William's son, Charles and behind William is his wife, Martha. (Courtesy of DPC.)

In 1907, the Civil War Monument seen above was dedicated by the General Reno Post 47 and the Woman's Relief Corps No. 14 at Greenwood Memorial Terrace. Several veterans and their wives attended the event, as Greenwood had the largest section of Union soldiers interred than any other cemetery in Washington. On Memorial Day 1921, veterans of the Grand Army of the Republic, Sedgwick Post, attended a ceremony at Greenwood Cemetery. Among the attendees in the photograph below, aged veteran Josephus Hobbs recalled seeing Abraham Lincoln in 1858 at the Stephen Douglas debates in Quincy, Illinois. "Lincoln was one of the greatest of the world's great men," Hobbs stated. Another veteran, Alonzo Moe, was one of the 128 Union soldiers who captured Jefferson Davis, president of the Confederacy. Moe was wounded and carried the bullet in his body until his death in 1939. (Above, courtesy of Rob Goff; below, courtesy of JQCPBCL.)

At the end of World War I, towns around the United States celebrated Armistice Day on November 11, 1918. The photograph above is taken of a parade with the boys marching home down spectator-lined Riverside Avenue in Spokane, Washington, as the band played "I Want to go Home." A Model T with a sailor sitting on the running board is parked in front of the Fern café. The nearby Rex Theater was screening the hit movie "Laughing Bill Hyde," starring Will Rogers and Mabel Ballin. In the photograph at right, Roy C. Seaver, a private once enlisted in Battery "F" 27th Artillery C.A.C. 46th Company 166th Depot Brigade, came home and was discharged November 16, 1918. Roy returned to his job as a telegraph operator and was issued a Bronze Victory Button. (Above, courtesy of NRSPL; below, courtesy of DPC.)

In the photograph at left, George Dittmar was mustered out of the United States Navy after World War I and returned to Spokane, where he owned a grocery store, the Cecil Apartments, and the Red Top Motel. Ted Spracklen entered the U.S. Army Air Forces in 1943. During World War II he served as a tail gunner, 18th Bomb Squadron, 34th Bomb Group along with his crew members, pictured below, from left to right: (standing) Rietman, engineer; Brown, bombardier; Johnson, copilot; Reed, navigator; and Hoffman, pilot; (kneeling) Unkleslee, armor left waist; Spracklen; Stone, armor right waist; MacFarland, lower ball; and Summers, radio operator. Ted was stationed in England and his plane was shot down on a flight over Russia; he was officially listed as MIA. Rescued and passed through Allied forces by way of Egypt, he finally arrived home six months later. Ted returned to logging and farming after the war. (Above, courtesy of DPC; below, courtesy of Evelyn Varga.)

In 1940, William Gabor Varga, a young man from New Jersey, came to the Northwest to work with the Civilian Conservation Corps (CCC). He met Shirley Spracklen in Couer d'Alene Park and they were married two months later. Drafted in 1943, "Bill," pictured at right, entered the Armored Tank Division, Company C, 812th Tank Battalion, M4A3 Sherman Tanks. Below is William with members of his battalion, from left to right: (first row) William, Kuznair, and Stump Frenchy; (sitting) Weynatcher, Hayes, and Buji. Bill was stationed in South Carolina, and when his mother died of cancer, he was granted leave. During that time, his unit was transferred overseas and all lost their lives in action. On Bill's return to duty, he was reassigned to a tank destroyer unit in Texas. After the war, he returned to Spokane to work and raise a family. (Courtesy of Evelyn Varga.)

Donald B. Popejoy Sr., pictured in the center, was inducted into the service March 27, 1944, and served overseas in the China Burma India (CBI) Theater with the 330th General Service Engineer Regiment. Don was a TEC/sergeant and was responsible for over 200 truck drivers, mechanics, dispatchers, repair specialists, and lubrication men while building the Ledo Road from India to China. Don was discharged May 29, 1946, and then joined the Regular Army as corporal until December 1948. (Courtesy of DPC.)

Above are the men of Company A of the 161st Infantry Division at Fort George Wright, Spokane. The three men in the front row are holding Browning Automatic Rifles (BAR), designed by Robert Browning in 1917. Fort Wright was officially opened in 1899, closed in 1957, and was named after Brig. Gen. George Wright, Union Army, during the American Civil War. (Courtesy of JQCPBCL.)

The first Declaration Day in Spokane was celebrated July 4, 1888. Leading the procession is the parade marshall, Frank Johnson, followed by several mounted dignitaries, along Second Avenue. As the procession heads toward its destination, the band and the American flag can be seen following the horsemen. Throughout the parade route, bystanders watched as the column of marching soldiers from Fort Spokane passed in review. As in all parades, this one seemed endless as the participants faded in the distance. (Courtesy of TCNRSPL.)

The Spokane Masonic Temple of Spokane, Washington, opened in August, 1905. Members of the regional Masonic organizations marched along Riverside Avenue to the Spokane Masonic Temple, which was dedicated June 14, 1906. The Masons wore their Masonic aprons as they entered the new facility, while the band, to the left, played patriotic music. (Courtesy of TCNRSPL.)

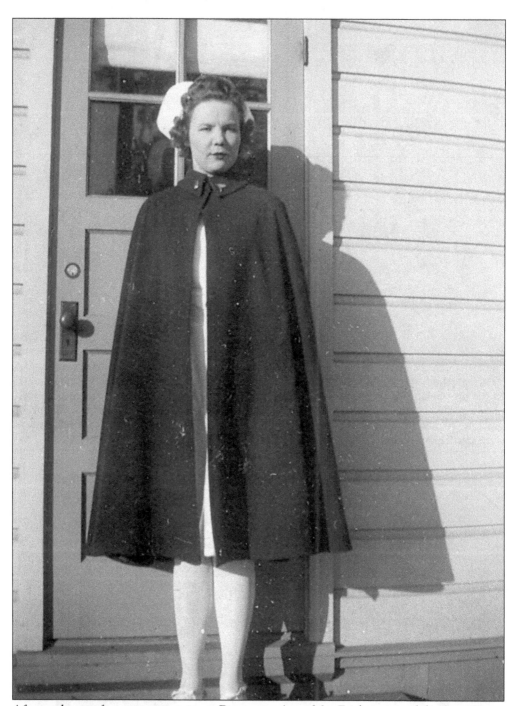

After graduating from nurses training at Deaconess, Anna Mae Ericksen joined the Army Nurse Corps and continued training at Fort Wright. "During field maneuvers, the soldiers would shout out flirting comments to the nurses," said Anna. She was stationed at Kelly Field near Antonio, Texas. Her most memorable patient was Max Baer, the Heavyweight Champion of the World. Anna recalls, "Max would call me ma while, following me during rounds, wearing polka dot pajamas and women's perfume." (Courtesy of Anna Mae Ericksen.)

Four

BRAVE MEN AND DEVOTED WOMEN

Harry Lillis (Bing) Crosby, the famous singer, was born May 3, 1903, in Tacoma, Washington, before moving to Spokane, where he grew up from the age of three. Before he was able to complete his study of law at Gonzaga University, he pursued a singing career. Gonzaga University is the home of the Bing Crosby Museum in the Foley Center. Mary Huetter McKee identified the home in the photograph above as belonging to her grandfather, John T. Huetter. Bing Crosby is sitting in the middle with a mitt between two unidentified boys. The children in the back, from left to right, are Francis Huetter, an unidentified boy, Paul J. Huetter, and Henry A. Huetter. (Courtesy of the Bing Crosby Collection, Gonzaga University Archives.)

The first bridge spanning the Spokane River was built in 1864. Michael Cowley bought the bridge in 1872, and built a trading post on the north side of the river. Cowley served as postmaster of Spokane Bridge from 1875 to 1879. This post office, the first in Spokane County, was active until 1958. Cowley's two-story house built in 1880, as seen above, sits on the north bank of the river and commanded a spectacular view. In 1887, he sold his property and moved into Spokan Falls. This photograph below of the Spokane River was taken in 1922 and shows the bridge that replaced Cowley's. This one was made of concrete and steel, and was used until 1950. The concrete pillars remain and the approaches to the bridge on the north bank, out of view to the right, can still be seen. (Above, courtesy of DPC; below, courtesy of TASBC.)

James Glover, known as the "Father of Spokane," arrived in Spokan Falls from Salem, Oregon, on May 11, 1873. Glover was searching for a location to build a town to be alongside the route of the transcontinental railroad. After his arrival, he bought prime property along the falls of the Spokane River. Susan Crump Glover, the first wife of James Glover, was "insane, found in a demented condition and placed in custody" according to *The Spokesman Review*. The article lists her as "formerly the wife of Councilman J.N. Glover." Susan was admitted to a mental hospital July 3, 1899. According to several sources, Susan was declared unfit by Glover, as she could not bear him children. Glover filed for divorce, and stated that Susan was "guilty of cruel treatment . . . and heaped personal indignation upon him," therefore he could not live with her. They were officially divorced March 31, 1892. As a part of the divorce, Glover provided Susan with a house in Oregon and gave her $100 a month. Many people sided with Susan in regards to their unhealthy marriage. Both died in 1921. (Above, courtesy of NRSPL; below, courtesy of TASBC.)

Two days after Glover's divorce from Susan, he married Ester "Etty" Leslie on April 2, 1892 and they moved into their new home. Glover's third home, designed by Spokane architect Kirtland Cutter and built in 1889, was an English-style mansion,. The house, pictured below, was made of local granite, carved woodwork from Minnesota, and furnishings from the east. The house had 22 rooms and 3 bathrooms, with inside plumbing! In the 1913 photograph above, James and Etty are seen sitting in the parlor, enjoying each other's company. (Above, courtesy of NRSPL; below, courtesy of BCNRSPL.)

In 1805, the Lewis and Clark Expedition came through Spokane Country, leaving behind a lasting legacy of their journey. One of the Corps members, Sgt. Patrick Gass, became a grandfather on February 3, 1877, when his daughter, Maria, gave birth to Benjamin Patrick Brierley. Patrick was born in Wellsburg, West Virginia, and worked as a traveling salesman for the Chicago Copy Company. Benjamin traveled all over the United States and arrived in Spokane on December 22, 1934. Patrick stayed at the Pennington Hotel and died in his room of acute alcoholism as certified by T. E. Barnhart, County Coroner on January 4, 1935. Brierley was buried in Evergreen Cemetery in Spokane, his marker pictured above. The old Pennington Hotel, below, was built in 1893 on the corner of Post and First Streets, next to the Hazelwood Dairy and Louis Davenport's Restaurant. (Above, courtesy of DPC; below, courtesy of ETBCNRSPL.)

The Nez Perce Indian War brought fear and possible danger throughout eastern Washington and in Spokan Falls during the summer of 1877. Frederick Dashiell, pictured with his wife Margaret, often brought supplies to Spokan Falls, along with lumber to James Glover's mill. According to family history, Fredrick encountered the Nez Perce and met Chief Joseph. The Dashiells became prominent in the farming community for several generations. (Courtesy of Tom and Artis Dashiell.)

James Glover worked hard convincing Frederick Post in relocating his Post Falls, flour mill to Spokane Falls in 1887. Post, his wife and five daughters were old country Germans who eventually accepted the offer of 40 acres of land. The property passed between Glover and Post five times, but the price always stayed the same. Post finally sold it to A. M. Cannon and J. J. Browne. Post Street was named after him. (Courtesy of NRSPL.)

58

Francis Cook was born in 1851, in Marietta, Ohio, and started his first newspaper at the age of 16. After moving to the west side of Washington, he became the owner of the *Olympia Echo* and the *Tacoma Herald*, eventually moving to Spokan Falls and establishing the *Spokan Times* newspaper on May 8, 1879. Francis Cook was one of the most important men in the shaping of Spokane, and lived in this nine-bedroom house on the South Hill next to Grand Avenue. He started the first steam motor trolley, called the Spokane and Montrose, in 1888; he owned the Montrose (Manito) Park Addition, Wandermere Lake, and Mt. Spokane road; and was known as the "Father of Mount Spokane State Park." He died June 29, 1920, leaving his wife and 11 children, but was remembered as a respectable and honorable man. (Above, courtesy of TASBC; below, courtesy of ETBCNRSPL.)

This house, located on the corner of Boone Avenue and Adams Streets, was built for Clark Boughton in 1887. Clark operated the C&C Flour Mill that was located where the Washington Water Power building is. His son, Joseph, owned the Keystone House and Falls View Hotel. Members of the Boughton family, seen below on the porch are, from left to right, Mrs. William Boughton, Amabell Boughton (sitting on the small chair), Mrs. Anna Hanson Boughton, Clark Boughton Sr., William Boughton and son Clark Boughton Jr. Clark and Anna Boughton had several children: Amos, Joseph, William, and Jennie, who is pictured at left. Jennie was in charge of the periodical room at the Spokane Public Library from 1902 through 1942. She was an accomplished writer and the author of *Spokane From Memory* and *Forty Years of Library Service*. She was the historian for the Spokane Pioneer's Society. (Courtesy of BCNRSPL.)

In 1887, Dr. Mary Latham was the first female doctor in the Washington Territory. She was a promoter of the library, the Horticultural Society, the Humane Society, and a writer. Spokane regarded her as a "patron saint," but after her son was killed, she committed a crime. Being convicted of arson, she escaped to Idaho as a wanted woman. After being apprehended, she spent a little over one year in prison, but was released early to practice medicine. She died in 1917. (Courtesy of Duane Broyles Fairmont Memorial Cemetery)

Mrs. Alice Houghton, born in Canada in 1849, was revered for her strong mind. In 1864, she married Horace E. Houghton, a practicing attorney and judge. In 1888, shortly after moving to Spokane Falls, she started the successful real estate, insurance and investments company, Mrs. Alice Houghton and Company. Alice had two children, Harry and Idell, but still found time to be a community leader. (Courtesy of NRSPL.)

Hiram Muzzy moved his family from New York to Spokane Falls to grow apples in 1880. He homesteaded Muzzy's Addition of 160 acres and later developed them. Hiram and Rebecca (Ames) Muzzy had five children: Nellie, Lewis, Alma, Lucy, and Frank. The Muzzy Mansion was later sold to Pat Shine, a prominent attorney and politician. Today the Muzzy Mansion Bed and Breakfast is owned by Mike Schultz and Steven Sanford and has been restored to replicate the feel of the 1880s (www.muzzymansion.com). Nellie (Muzzy) Mills, shown at left, married Barton Mills, and homesteaded a farm on Newman Lake. When Barton was shot by claim jumpers, Nellie's Brother Frank bought the preemption rights from Nellie. Nellie was one of the first teachers in Spokane and taught at the Bancroft school. (Above, courtesy of Muzzy Mansion; below, courtesy of NRSPL.)

Helga Estby (sitting, at right) and her daughter, Clara, walked across America in 1896 to win a wager of $10,000 in New York City. Unfortunately, they were a few days late and never received the prize. The story was forgotten, until Linda Lawrence Hunt discovered an essay by Doug Bahr about his great-great-grandmother. Linda retold this incredible story in her book *Bold Spirit*. Helga, 36, and Clara, 18, left their family farm in Mica Creek May 5, 1896, on an adventure that would last seven months. All they brought with them was $10, a Smith and Wesson revolver, red pepper spray (for dangerous animals), a compass, a map, a few medical supplies, a lantern for night walking, photographs of themselves they planned to sell to help fund their expedition, a curling iron and a letter of introduction by Mayor Belt of Spokane. Above is the Estby home on the corner of Helena Street and Mallon Avenue. The family members are, from left to right, Ida, Olaf (seated), William, Lillian, Helga, and Arthur. (Courtesy of the Dorothy and Daryll Bahr collection.)

KIRTLAND KELSEY CUTTER
Architect. Born Cleveland, Ohio, August 20, 1860.
Arrived in Washington October 1886. Address,
Spokane, Wash.

Kirtland Kelsey Cutter was one of Spokane's most famous architects. Since leaving Cleveland for Spokane in 1886, a number of the beautiful Browne's Addition mansions exhibit his distinctive touch. Some of the homes Cutter designed in the Browne's Addition Neighborhood belonged to Patsy Clark, John Finch, Robert Strahorn, Jay Graves and Cowles. His commercial works of art include the Davenport Hotel, the Spokane Club, the First National Bank, the White House Store and many others. (Courtesy of NRSPL.)

John Aylard Finch, born in England in 1854, was known as one of Spokane's greatest philanthropists. Kirtland Cutter built his Georgian Revival mansion on First Street, a few doors from the Campbell mansion. John and his wife, Charlotte, made their fortune through Finch and Campbell Mining Company, White and Bender Company, Blalock Fruit Company, Coeur d'Alene Hardware Company, and the National Lumber Company. The Finch Arboretum is a wonderful tribute to him. (Courtesy of NRSPL.)

Father's Day was created by Sonora Smart Dodd (above) after her mother's death, leaving her father, William Smart (below), to raise her and five younger brothers. Sonora thought the world of her father. "He was a Golden Rule Type of Father," said told the *Spokane Chronicle* in an interview from June 6, 1910. Her idea came from a sermon she heard about Mother's Day and she thought Fathers deserved to be honored the same way. With the help of her minister, she established Father's Day on June 19, 1910. In 1924, Pres. Calvin Coolidge shared it with the nation. Pres. Lyndon Johnson publicly recognized Sonora's idea in 1966, which was soon followed by President Nixon signing a proclamation permanently observing Father's Day in 1972. Today over 50 countries annually celebrate Father's Day on the third Sunday of June. (Courtesy of NRSPL.)

Martha Canary, better known as "Calamity Jane," actually "dealt faro bank on Main Avenue in a wooden building that stood adjacent to what is now the Owl saloon" in the early 1880s, according to the *Spokane Press* on August 6, 1903. She became famous for assisting General Custer in the Indian battles; she wore men's clothes and could drink with the best of them. She was in Deadwood when Wild Bill Hickok was shot and was later buried next to him. (Courtesy of TCNRSPL.)

Gladys Spracklen met Buffalo Bill Cody while working in a restaurant in Wyoming. She and her family moved to the Northwest after the "dust bowl," where they owned a ranch with sheep, cattle, and horses. Gladys always dressed-up when riding, sometimes donning sheep wool chaps as in the picture above. Her love of horses inspired her to ride everyday, until an injury prevented her from riding at the age of 85. In 2000, Gladys died at the age of 105. (Courtesy of Evelyn Varga (1895–2000).)

Butch Cassidy, at right, died in a shootout in Bolivia in November 1908. However, a rumor persists that Butch escaped, made his way to America and assumed the name William Philips, who is pictured below. William Philips moved to Spokane in 1910 and by 1911 he was second vice president to American Stereotypewriter Company and an engineer for the Washington Water Power Company. William was an inventor, designing the Philips Adding Machine and a garage-door opener. By 1918, William owned his own manufacturing company and a machine shop located at 1612 North Monroe. At the time, he lived in a house under the Highbridge Railroad trestle. In 1925, William worked for the Riblet Tramway Company and moved to a spacious and elegantly furnished home. Phillips wrote a book called *The Bandit Invincible: The Story of the Outlaw Butch Cassidy*. He became indigent and was sent to Broadacres in Spangle for care and treatment, where he died in 1937. (Above, courtesy of Utah State Historical Society; below, courtesy of the Larry Pointer Collection, Box 22, American Heritage Center, University of Wyoming.)

Spokane owes a debt of gratitude to Charles Augustus Libby Sr. and Jr. for preserving history through photography. Charles Sr. started his photography business on Post Street in 1898, but moved several times. Charles Jr., a major in the Army Air Corps during World War II, started as a photography instructor, and then he captured aerial films for the army, navy, and marines. He was stationed at the Pentagon in Washington, D.C. Charles Sr. and his son's photographs of Spokane span from 1898 to 1961. They produced the largest mural in the Northwest, 9-feet-by-19-feet, for the Elks lodge in Spokane. In 1967, they were given the Professional Photographers of America award for distinguished service. Charles Sr. died in 1966, and Charles Jr. died in 1982. The picture below is of Gretchen Libby (married to Charles Libby Sr.), at right, and Florence Hafer, at left. Charles F. Hafer took this picture at Hayden Lake. Like Charles Sr. and Charles Jr., he had a passion for photography. (Above, courtesy of JQCPBCL; below, courtesy of Virginia Adsit.)

Levi Hutton was an engineer on the Northern Pacific railroad and lived at May Arkwright's boardinghouse in Idaho. They fell in love, and shortly after their marriage, they combined incomes to buy a share of the Hercules mine. The Hercules mine paid off very well and they became millionaires. May Hutton was always concerned for the rights of women workers and children ever since she met President McKinley as a child, who told her, "I hope that one day you might live and vote under equal suffrage." When the Huttons moved to Spokane, they built a large downtown building and a beautiful home on the south hill. May became actively involved with the women's suffrage movement and several other causes. She was the first woman to attend the Democratic Convention. The picture below is of Levi Hutton on the tractor, plowing the earth, and the picture at right shows May Arkwright Hutton. (Above, courtesy of Museum of Arts and Culture, Hutton Settlement Collection, photograph L94-9.1; below, courtesy of JQCPBCL.)

Levi Hutton's wife, May, passed away from Bright's disease in 1915. After May's death, Levi pursued his dream of building a children's home. Levi Hutton had himself been an orphan and had a great desire to help children in the same situation. The Hutton Settlement Children's Home was built in 1919 from his vision and the help of architect Harold C. Whitehouse. The farm was self-supporting, and the children learned values of living in the country. Even though Levi died November 3, 1928, the Hutton Settlement continues to help children. The picture above is of a Christmas program for the children, with Levi in the center. Below is a photograph of the Settlement children getting haircuts. (Courtesy of JQCPBCL.)

The Aslin-Finch Company was listed in Polk's Directory of 1938 as one of 19 retail feed dealers and one wholesale outfit. Fred Aslin and Jack Finch purchased the property from James Keeth on May 31, 1938. The original building was located at 1827 East Sprague, but when Keeth raised the price, Aslin and Finch moved one block west to 1821 East Sprague, as seen above. The Aslin-Finch store sold feed, hay, grain, seed, fertilizer, along with poultry and dairy products. In between the customers' visits, Jack and Fred swept up the delivery room, shown at right at the double back door. In 1974, Aslin sold his company, which has retained its original name. The feed store eventually became the home of the Standard Plumbing and Heating Company. (Courtesy of Will Aslin.)

These lively ladies are all dressed up and ready for Easter. From their hats and bonnets to their frilly dresses, they are eager to celebrate spring. The women are, from left to right, Helen Jacobson, Dorothy Osborne, Janice Huckley, and Hazel Haynes. In this era, ladies often spent afternoons enjoying tea, cakes, and good company. If the hostess was not home during a customary visit, a decorative visiting card was left on a tray in the parlor. Don Popejoy Sr. and his little brother Roy seem to be all dressed up with no place to go. Note the fancy sailor suit and double buckle shoes with white stockings that Don is wearing. Small children like Roy, were usually dressed alike until age four to six, when the boys were "breeched" (put into breeches after being in petticoats from birth.) (Courtesy of DPC.)

Five

RIVERSIDE AND MAIN

Spokane shows off its splendor in this 1915 image. In the center, the Spokesman Review Building, built in 1891, is an exquisite example of Romanesque architecture. The statue of Ensign John Monaghan was erected in 1906. Monaghan lost his life saving a wounded soldier in Samoa during the Spanish-American War. The Red Crown Standard Oil Company was owned by Richard Sawyer and sold gas for 14¢ a gallon. (Courtesy of JQCPBCL.)

This photograph shows the original Monroe Bridge over the Spokane River, built in 1889, and destroyed by fire in 1890. Note the electric trolley and horse drawn carriage. This 1930s view features the city's skyline and some of its landmarks. East from Peaceful Valley along the Spokane River is the Spokane Casket Company, in the lower right of the photograph. The road to the right is Main Street, which leads to the Monroe Street Bridge, built in 1911, and into the heart of downtown Spokane. From left to right is the Great Northern Depot Clock Tower and Railroad Bridge crossing above the Monroe Street Bridge, built in 1892; Montgomery Ward's, built in 1929; The Spokesmen Review Tower, built in 1891; the spires of the Cathedral of Our Lady of Lourdes, built in 1903; and the twin stacks of the Heat, Light, and Power Company's steam plant, built in 1916. (Courtesy of TCNRSPL, photograph by Charles Libby.)

August 4, 1889, was the date of Spokane's Great Fire. There have been several accounts of how it actually started: Some say it started in the kitchen of Wolfe's Lunch Counter from grease igniting, while others say it started from a grass fire in the alley behind. No one is sure, but they do know that the city water manager, Rolla A. Jones, was off on a fishing trip and no one knew how to run the system. He was later exonerated. All the buildings were lost from the Northern Pacific freight building north to Havermale Island and from Lincoln street going east to Washington. The firemen worked hard trying to stop the fire by setting off dynamite around the burning area, only to have it jump the fire line. People and supplies came by train from numerous towns throughout the Inland Northwest to help Spokane. Fort Spokane and Fort Sherman both sent tents and guardsmen to place Spokane under military law. The tents pictured above are of J. C. Eaton's Men's Furnishings and the Clough and Graves Real Estate Bank. The picture below is of John Graham's Books, News and Stationery. (Above, courtesy of TCNRSPL; below, courtesy of ETBCNRSPL.)

Fortunately, the Crescent department store did not burn, and the town's citizens were able to buy the supplies they needed to restart their lives. The view above is facing east along Sprague Avenue from Lincoln Street. *The Chronicle* was able to use an old handpress from across the river to get the newspaper out the next day. The *New York Times* also covered the fire. By the next day, business started again, but this time in tents. During reconstruction, Spokane had a large gulley by the river, where the library stands today. The gulley was filled with the fire debris. Below is a photograph of various businesses forced to temporarily operate out of tents, including a railroad ticket sales outfit; Clothing House; The White House; A. W. Siegel; Frankfurt Beer, Cigars, and Tobacco; and Dutch Jake's Beer Garden. Spokane had only one fire related death, and the town quickly rebuilt into a prosperous city. (Above, courtesy of NRSPL; below, courtesy of JQCPBCL.)

This picture amplifies the tragic state of Spokane as fire adjusters gathered to sort through all the claims after the Fire of 1889. The *New York Times* stated that $2,350,000 was paid in insurance claims. The man in the background wearing a chef's hat is Joseph Pellanda. (Courtesy of TCNRSPL.)

Louis Davenport wanted to be sure that every detail of his hotel was of the highest quality. He controlled his own water supply, steam powered generator, dairy farm, and even a chicken ranch in Deer Park. John Fahey wrote, "Near Deer Park, Louis M. Davenport maintained a chicken farm, managed by an Arcadia tract buyer, Felix Veran, to produce 2,400 eggs a day for his famed Spokane restaurant," in the Fahey Papers of the Northwest Room at the Spokane Public Library. (Courtesy of the Lawrence Zimmerer Collection.)

Spring of 1889 would bring Spokane Falls into the age of elegance with the arrival of Lewellyn "Louis" Davenport from San Francisco to work at his uncle's restaurant. His work was disrupted by the Great Fire of August 1889, when most of downtown was destroyed. His entrepreneurial side emerged and he raised a tent, establishing Davenport's Waffle Foundry. It grew into a restaurant and he eventually bought the Belview Block, which his sister-in-law, Maude Pennington, operated for him. In 1908, Louis had asked Kirtland Cutter to design one of the finest hotels in the west. The Davenport Hotel, a Mission Revival design, opened September 19, 1914, with all the elegance of Europe. Will Rogers, Bing Crosby, Mary Pickford, Clark Gable, Bob Hope, Benny Goodman, Douglas Fairbanks, Ethel Barrymore, Babe Ruth, Joe Louis, Charles Lindbergh, Amelia Earhart, Theodore Roosevelt, John F. Kennedy, and many other dignitaries were among those to experience Spokane's finest. (Above, courtesy of NRSPL; below, courtesy of the Ethel White Collection, NRSPL.)

Davenport's Restaurant, Spokane, Wash.

The Davenport Hotel had the finest ballrooms, with names such as the Marie Antoinette Ballroom, Elizabethan Banquet Room, Isabella Room, Georgian Room, Mandarin Room, Circus Room (designed for Harper Joy, a circus lover and friend of Louis Davenport), and the Hall of Doges, named after the Palace of Doges in Venice. Every need was assigned a shop, whether it be sports, delicacy, pharmaceuticals, jewelers, library, flowers, housewares, watches, barber, travel, Great Northern train tickets, bowling alley, or photographers. The hotel even had its own band; it was like a city within a city. The front lobby welcomed customers with fish aquariums and a pond. The food was, and still is, an epicurean delight. (Courtesy of JQCPBCL.)

James P. McGoldrick married Eliza McArdle, of St. Paul Minnesota in 1888, and they had five children: Edward, Carroll, Milton, Margaret, and Helen. In 1905, he bought A. M. Fox's lumber company in Spokane, just south of Gonzaga University, and relocated his lumber enterprise from Minnesota. In fact, McGoldrick lumber leased land from Gonzaga University, benefitting both parties. It was the largest employer in Spokane for many years. James McGoldrick bought a large tract of land in Kootenai County, Idaho for logging, and later sold the land to people to start their homes. The logs were sent down the St. Marie River, to St. Joes River, onward to Lake Coeur d'Alene, and then to the OWR&N Railroad, going south of Mica hill to Spokane. The picture below shows the log pond with the "big burner" built in 1909. (Courtesy of NRSPL.)

The picture above is of the McGoldrick planning mill, and the brick building housed the steam boilers. Below is the McGoldrick dump truck that was used to haul shavings to places like Sacred Heart Hospital for heating. James McGoldrick built a railroad line known as the Hangman Creek Railroad, which ran many spurs to service a large area of logging. He was the founder of the Inland Empire Safety Council, and director of the Old National Bank, among other enterprises. His third generation, James P. McGoldrick, followed in his grandfather's footsteps, learning the lumber business, and later started his own business. He is an accomplished pilot and the writer of two books, *The McGoldrick Lumber Company Story, 1900–1952* and the *Spokane Aviation Story, 1910–1941*. In 1945, a huge fire destroyed the lumber mill and eventually closed for business on May 4, 1946. (Courtesy of JQCPBCL.)

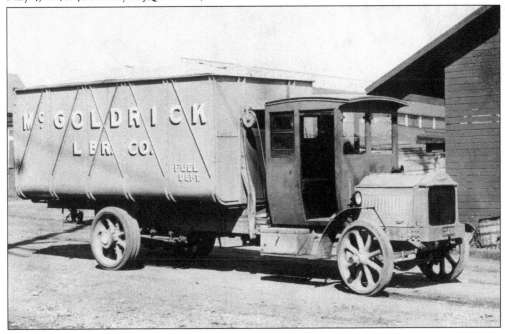

Willis A. Richey, a new arrival to Spokane, designed the Spokane County Courthouse in 1893. With just a course outlined by the superintendent of architecture from the U.S. Treasury, Richey won the competition for one of Spokane's finest landmarks. He had designed many public buildings including the onetime state capital in Thurston County, Washington. Mayor David B. Fothingtham was the contractor, and he finished building the French Renaissance courthouse in 1895. (Courtesy of JQCPBCL.)

The view in this photograph is from the Spokesman-Review Building on Riverside Street in 1930. To the left is post office. The first post office started in Spokane Falls July 5, 1872, with Seth R. Scranton as the first postmaster. A little farther down the street is the Libby Photography building. Charles Libby and his son played a large role in documenting much of Spokane's history. (Courtesy of JQCPBCL.)

Clarence Dill was known as the "Grandfather of Grand Coulee Dam" for bringing the dam to the attention of Franklin D. Roosevelt. Clarence Dill, born in Ohio, September 21, 1884, married Mabel Dixon Dill, founder of the home economics department at Whitworth College. Dill practiced law in Spokane between serving as a member of the House of Representatives for two terms from 1915 to 1919, followed by two terms in the U.S. Congress from 1923 to 1935. (Courtesy of Maxine Olsen.)

Spokane Casket Company was established by Smith Funeral Home in 1899. Located at 1610–1620 Water Avenue in Peaceful Valley, it was one of the largest casket companies serving Washington, Idaho, Montana, and Utah. The business so profitable, it expanded in 1913 while under George Clark's management, but later was demolished in 1999. (Courtesy of NRSPL.)

The hardware enterprise Jensen, Brooke, and company started in Sprague in 1883. It later merged with another company and changed location to Riverside Avenue, Spokane, under the name Jensen-Byrd. It is now one of the largest independent wholesalers in the country. (Courtesy of JQCPBCL.)

At the time this photograph was taken, the Rex Theater was screening the 1908 movie, *The Call of the Wild*, adapted from Jack London's 1903 adventure book. The film, directed by D.W. Griffith, starred Charles Inslee, Harry Solter, and Florence Lawrence. The Pathé Newsreel signs are visible in the front. Shown at movies between 1910 and 1956, Pathé Newsreels were initially presented as silent films, before incorporating voiceover narration in the 1930s. (Courtesy of JQCPBCL.)

Jimmy Durkin, a shrewd saloon owner, was one of Spokane's wealthiest residents. His 1934 grave marker offers the epitaph, "He is a man of his word," referring to a promise he made to a Baptist minister that was granted permission to decorate the windows of his saloon with anti-drinking propaganda. This turned out to be great publicity for Durkin and his business. He also had these words on the wall of his saloon: "If children need shoes don't buy booze." He was regarded as a very open-minded man and even wrote a letter to Clarence Darrow during the Scopes evolution trial, congratulating him for using freedom of thought and education when he was defending Scopes against William Jennings Bryan. Durkin ran for as a Democratic candidate for governor in 1908, but lost in the primary. He was a millionaire, but left the liquor business in 1915 to abide with Prohibition. (Courtesy of ETBCNRSPL.)

FRANK BOHM PRESENTS

DEIRO

THE MASTER OF THE PIANO ACCORDION

MAE
WEST

"THE ORIGINAL BRINKLEY GIRL"

LOEW CIRCUIT

SEASON 1916-17
MUSICAL COMEDY

WISHING THE ENTIRE WORLD A MERRY XMAS AND A HAPPY NEW YEAR

Guido Diero, the accordion master, played at the Orpheum Theatre in Spokane in 1913. He had a romantic encounter with a local pianist, Julia Tatro, and even though she was not with child, her family insisted on marriage. After the wedding, Guido returned to his travels. In February 1914, Guido was arrested in Chicago for not financially supporting Julia, though the charges were eventually dropped. That incident was followed by a divorce in the summer of 1914. Guido then quickly married his long time girlfriend, Mae West, a young vaudeville star. It was later she became the widely recognized film actress and sex symbol, as she is remembered today. (Courtesy of Count Guido Diero.)

The Washington Confectionery Shop sat at the corner of Washington Street and Fourth Avenue. In the photograph, Don Popejoy Sr. has just lowered the awning and is ready for business. On both side of the shop are ads for Pepsi-Cola and Coca-Cola. There are signs for Philip Morris cigarettes, Hi-Hat ice cream cones for 5¢ (the price in 1914), aviation gifts, and model figures with the ad reading "Did you say 10¢?" Inside the doors are bar stools, a counter, and a milk shake machine, which is visible in the window. (Courtesy of DPC.)

Prior to the advent of chain stores, family-owned businesses flourished. As seen in the 1920s photograph at right, this local grocery store stocks both staple and fancy products. Elmer Helm, proprietor, and his father-in-law Addison Haynes, are ready for another day's work. The two advertisements are for London Life cigarettes, founded in 1892 by S. Anargyros in New York City, consisting of straight Turkish tobacco; and for Star Tobacco Company, based in Irvington, New Jersey. The photograph below of a 1930s vintage dry goods store located on Main Street sold products such as candy, laundry soap, lard, coffee, bags of flour, and featured a butcher counter. The photograph shows Jack Marley, the butcher; Mark Moulton; Tom Smart; George Dittmar, the owner; and Jess Carlton, in "the cage" above. Note the lady to the right, wearing a fashionable bonnet. (Courtesy of DPC.)

Pat Thompson stands on the corner of Eighth Avenue and Washington Street in front of Parabola apartments, which her mother Hazel (Parker) Sandholm converted from the Heiberg Estate into separate living quarters. Dr. B. F. Burch, married to Laura Havermale (daughter of Rev. Samuel Havermale), built the home before the 1889 fire. Many of the residents of downtown used the house as a refuge during the fire. The 22-room mansion was described as a storybook, enchanted palace. The Paragon dress store, owned by Hazel Sandholm, was located across the street from the Davenport Hotel. Pat Thompson remembers Bing Crosby's mother having her hair done in the upstairs beauty salon that was part of the dress shop. (Courtesy of Pat Thompson.)

Six

SERVING SPOKANE

In 1936, Harold Van Horne began delivering mail by way of a pony cart on the Hillyard route. There were few horse and cart routes in the United States, but Spokane had six of them. According to Harold's wife, Evelyn Van Horne, "In 1953, Harold became a postmaster in Elk until he retired in 1972." (Courtesy of JQCPBCL.)

Sitting to the left is Peter Mertz, Spokane's sixth police chief. The man on the right, Chief Phillip Gough, was an inspector working for Peter Mertz. Below is a photograph of the police department taken August 1894. They are, from left to right, as follows: (first row) Peter R. Nimes, Dougald D. McPhee, Thomas M. Lothrop, Silas S. Parmeter, and William Shannon; (second row) Charles E. Owen, Dennis J. Sheehan, L. M. Larson, Robert A. Wilson, Harry Piper, and DeLano Davenport; (third row) William D. Nelson, Inspector Phil G. Gough, Chief Peter Mertz, Police Commissioner Frank Kizer, Henry C. Roff, and jailer Joe Rudersdorf; (fourth row) Burnham D. Brockman, Jerry B. Dunn, Sgt. William H. McKernan, Capt. James R. Coverly, Sgt. Charles Barlow, Otto Bringgold, and license inspector George Hollway; (fifth row) John T. Sullivan, William Smith, Dan Fisher, and Dan J. McMillan. This information is from *Life Behind the Badge: The Spokane Police Department's Founding Years, 1881–1903* by Suzanne and Tony Bamonte with the Spokane Police Department History Book Committee. (Above, courtesy of ETBCNRSPL; below, courtesy of JQCPBCL.)

This 1889 picture shows the building that housed the Spokane Fire Department and Police Department. City hall, not seen here, is located behind the Fire and Police side on Howard and Front Street. The Fire Department and Police Department wagons were horse-drawn in the early days. (Courtesy of Carolyn Nunemaker, NRSPL.)

The Hawthorne school built in 1898 was named after Nathaniel Hawthorne and demolished to build I-90. The identified students of the 1929 second grade class are, from left to right, as follows: (first row) Alex Nagahama, three unidentified students, George Shirago, Tom Kadoya, Harry Day, Doris Whitter, Toyo Migaki, Carol Donovan, Katherine Day, unidentified, Hisahi Takami, and Dick Yamamoto; (second row) Floyd, unidentified, Ray Ramsey, unidentified, Gordon, unidentified, Bonnie, unidentified, and Patsy Parker; (third row) all unidentified; (fourth row) unidentified, Isabella Cook, unidentified, Bernice Shafer, Jeanette Dayton, and three unidentified students. (Courtesy of Pat Thompson.)

The Irving Elementary School of Spokane, named for Washington Irving, opened in 1890. It was located on West 1716 Seventh Avenue. During its time in Spokane, the Irving school was a showplace with beautiful offices and classrooms, as can be seen by the wall decorations in this classroom. The Irving school pioneered a program for the deaf, and many children learned sign language. (Courtesy of NRSPL.)

The Lincoln School, named in honor of Pres. Abraham Lincoln, educated pupils from kindergarten through the 12th grade and was known to have a multicultural enrollment. It was designed by the Wells and Bertelsen architectural firm and built in 1888 by Larson Brothers Contractors. The school closed in 1967. (Courtesy of JQCPBCL.)

The Hillyard High School was built in 1907, named after railroad magnate James J. Hill, during a time when Hillyard was a town. In 1932, it was annexed into Spokane and later that year, a new school was built, John Rodgers High School, named for John R. Rodgers, the third governor of Washington State. (Courtesy of JQCPBCL.)

The Lewis and Clark High School was named after the Lewis and Clark expedition. The school started in 1890 as Spokane High School, then was renamed South Central High in 1908. On April 8, 1911, Pres. Theodore Roosevelt laid the cornerstone of the new Lewis and Clark High School. (Courtesy of NRSPL.)

Spokane College was built on 157 acres just north of the Spokane River and opened in October 1882. One of the founders was Col. David Jenkins, a Civil War veteran. When the college closed in October 1891, Colonel Jenkins founded Jenkins College that December, but then shut it down just six months later in 1892. The second Spokane College, as seen below, was established in 1909 on the east 700 block on Twenty-ninth Avenue, closed in 1929, and then was occupied by Spokane Junior College from 1935 to 1942. During World War II, the buildings became housing for soldiers stationed at Fort George Wright. The beautiful edifice was razed in 1969, and is now the site of Manito Shopping Center. (Above, courtesy of JQCPBCL; below, courtesy of Aage Anderson.)

George F. Whitworth (1816–1907) had a dream of a coeducational Presbyterian Christian College. His vision came to fruition south of Tacoma in 1890, and then moved to Spokane in 1914. Jay Graves, the railroad and real estate developer, donated land for the campus. It became Whitworth University in 2007, offering professional courses in art, science and studies of the Bible. The university was closed from 1918 until 1919, during which time is was used by the government at some stage in World War I. (Courtesy of Whitworth University Archives, Spokane, Washington.)

This 1892 picture was taken shortly after Fr. Joseph Cataldo founded Gonzaga College. The building was moved in 1900, only 500 feet to the east, to a quieter location. It was built for the Jesuits to continue educating the Indians. There are many important landmarks located on campus, including the St. Aloysius Church, built in 1911; the Foley Library; and the Bing Crosby Museum. In 1912, Gonzaga became a university. (Courtesy of Gonzaga University Archives.)

Sacred Heart Hospital was founded in 1886 by Mother Joseph, head of the Sisters of Providence. She was known as the first architect of the Northwest. After arriving from Vancouver, she began the design and construction of missions and hospitals to assist the less fortunate. Sacred Heart Hospital, built on land bought from S. G. Havermale, on Spokane Falls Boulevard, opened January 27, 1887, and later moved to the present location, 101 West Eighth Avenue. (Courtesy of Sacred Heart Medical Center and Children's Hospital.)

Bertha Turner, Sally Rutter, and Imogene Stone established St. Luke's Hospital on Sept. 2, 1897. The three women, who were members of All Saints Episcopal Cathedral, donated $900 to start the Spokane Protestant Sanatorium at the corner of Sprague and Madison. John A. Finch donated 12 lots to have it rebuilt in 1910, at a cost of $80,000. The hospital also housed a training school for nurses. (Courtesy of NRSPL.)

In 1896, deaconess Miss Clara Brown conceived the idea of another hospital for Spokane. Deaconess Hospital began in a few rented rooms in a building on Brown and Third Avenue. ,"A few days after its opening, the first operation was performed, with a breakfast table serving as an operating table, and a wash boiler as a sterilizer for the instruments." the *Spokane Daily Chronicle* reported on January 26, 1933. (Courtesy of JQCPBCL.)

Anna Mae Ericksen graduated from Deaconess Hospital School of Nursing in 1943. After returning from duty as an army nurse, she became head nurse in the emergency ward at Deaconess. The founder of the Washington State Poison Center, Anna Mae has continued to make Spokane a better community. She has been named Spokane Woman of Achievement, noted in *Who's Who of American Women* and invited to the White House to speak about emergency services. (Courtesy of Anna Mae Ericksen.)

The Red Cross is always there to help in times of need. On October 30, 1918, during the flu epidemic, the Red Cross organized a group of women to sew flu masks. The Old National Bank offered their building to the Red Cross as a provisional base of operations. Anna Mae Erickensen was a member for 67 years. The Anna Mae Ericksen Award is given every year to a rural nurse involved in the Inland Northwest Chapter of the American Red Cross. (Courtesy of JQCPBCL.)

In April 1939, the Pacific Telegraph and Telephone Company held a farewell party for the accounting department manager, the woman in the center of the photograph above. In the back row, third from the left, is Elaine Haynes, and second row left is her sister, Cleo Helms. Notice the elegant work clothes with feminine styling—a backlash to the boyish fashions of the Roaring Twenties—the upswept hairstyles, and artful makeup with pencil thin brows. In December 1886, Thomas Elsom, pictured at left, installed Spokane's first telephone set at a store located on the corner of Howard and Riverside. In 1915, the Pacific Company bought the local Spokane Company and changed the name to Pacific Telephone and Telegraph. In the 1920s, businesses only had one phone number and the calls were transferred by an operator to each office via the switchboard. Automatic switching was later developed to decrease costs. (Above, courtesy of DPC; below, courtesy of TASBC.)

Seven

ALL ABOARD

In 1887, one of the large clouds hanging over Spokane during the expansion of the railways was the fight against unjust freight rates of the Interstate Commerce Commission. On March 20, 1908, W. H. Cowles wrote letters to Pres. Theodore Roosevelt, soliciting his help. In this picture, Roosevelt is giving a speech addressing the Inland Empire Railway. Spokane finally prevailed 49 years later in the battle for fair railroad rates. (Courtesy of JQCPBCL.)

James Jerome Hill (September 16, 1838–May 29, 1916) was known as the "Empire Builder." On July 2, 1864, he began work on the Great Northern Railway without the use of the Pacific Railroad Act. He approached Spokane businessmen with the proposal to come into downtown at Havermale Island. He proclaimed if they could get the land, he would give them a fair deal, better than the other railroads. In his pursuit to acquire donations of land, Hill ended up deceiving the people of Spokane. James Hill declared, "Give me snuff, whiskey and Swedes, and I will build a railroad to hell." Below, the Great Northern Railway Depot, built in 1902, was known as one of the best depots west of Chicago. The depot was demolished to make room for the 1974 World's Fair. The clock tower, preserved as a reminder of earlier times, still stands in Riverfront Park today. (Above, courtesy of NRSPL; below, courtesy of JQCPBCL.)

Daniel Chase Corbin arrived in Spokane at 53 years of age in 1889. His wife, Louise Jackson Corbin, remained in England due to health issues. His son, Austin Corbin, was the only child that joined him in Spokane. His daughter latter married architect Kirtland Cutter, and they had a son, Kirtland Corbin Cutter. Daniel Corbin offered to help his daughter raise her son after her divorce from Cutter, with the stipulation that his name be changed to Corbin Corbin. Daniel Corbin's accomplishments were many: He built a concentrator mill for Bunker Hill and Sullivan mines, as well as started the Spokane Falls and Idaho Railway, and established the Coeur d'Alene Railway and Navigation Company, that linked up with the steamships from Lake Coeur d'Alene. Shown below is an advertisement for a trip to St. Maries on the Idaho Steamship. After much success, Daniel Corbin built a line to Colville, named the Spokane Falls and Northern Railroad, which eventually continued to Nelson B.C. In 1905, he built the Spokane International Railway to connect with the Canadian Pacific Railway. His other interests were varied: the Spokane Valley irrigation, sugar beets, mining and acting as a trustee for a bank. After he underwent a surgical procedure that resulted in pneumonia, Corbin passed away in 1918. (Above, courtesy of NRSPL; below, courtesy of JQCPBCL.)

SPECIAL MIDWEEK

Excursion to St. Maries

The steamer "Idaho" will make a special round trip to St. Maries up the

Beautiful Shadowy St. Joe River

Thursday, August 2

affording an excellent opportunity for spending the day on lake and river, as well as a charming ride over the cool, clean and comfortable Coeur d'Alene electric line.
Take the "Shoshone Flyer" leaving Spokane electric terminal at 7:50 a. m., returning to Spokane at 6:30 in the evening.

ROUND TRIP $2.00

Special Notice—An extra steamer will return from St. Maries after the ball game Thursday between Coeur d'Alene and St. Maries.

Jay Graves (1859–1948), his wife Amanda Cox, and son Clyde arrived in Spokane in 1887. Graves, a true entrepreneur at heart, brought along his partner, Charles F. Clough, to start the real estate firm of Clough and Graves. Among an enormous amount of accomplishments, he was the president of a title company; director of the Old National Bank; owner of the Granby mine. He acquired Montrose Park Addition, known today as South Hill; purchased the Spokane and Montrose motorized Streetcar from Francis Cook after the 1893 panic, then named his street car system the Spokane Traction Company; brought Aubrey White to Spokane; obtained the Coeur d'Alene and Spokane Railway, as seen below, which led to the Spokane and Inland Empire Railroad; donated the land for Whitworth College and what eventually became Manito Park; operated one of the most successful dairy farms; built Waikiki with architect Kirtland Cutter in the area of the Wandermere Golf course, which was landscaped by the Olmsted brothers; and finally, built the Nine Mile power generating plant. (Above, courtesy of NRSPL; below, courtesy of JQCPBCL.)

Robert Strahorn was the public relations man for the Union Pacific Railroad. His wife, Carrie Adell Strahorn, accompanied him, traveling by stage, horseback, and train and writing about the West in 1877, which led to her book about their travels, *Fifteen Thousand Miles by Stage*. Robert Strahorn was given the name "Railroad Sphinx," due to secret backing from Edward Harriman on his railroad, which became the Oregon-Washington Railroad and Navigation Company. The Strahorns bought J. J. Browne's home, built by Kirtland Cutter. (Courtesy of NRSPL.)

The Spokane and Inland Empire Railroad, organized by Jay Graves in 1904, changed its name to the Spokane, Coeur d'Alene and Palouse Railway in 1927, following the takeover by the Great Northern Railway. (Courtesy of NRSPL.)

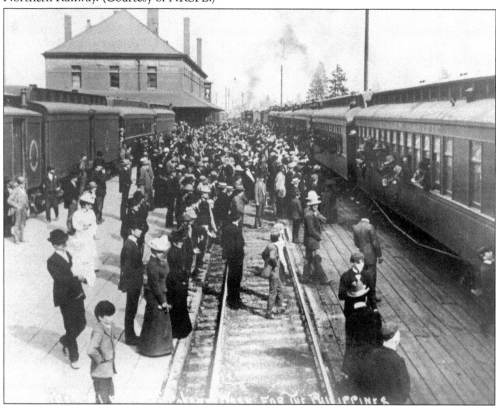

The Philippine War of Independence started for America on April 25, 1898, when President McKinley called for 125,000 volunteers to fight. Many were volunteers from Inland Empire. Within a few days, Spokane rallied to help. The town decorated Riverside with red, white, and blue to celebrate their heroes going off to war. In this picture they are waving good-bye to the soldiers from the Northern Pacific Train Depot. (Courtesy of JQCPBCL.)

In 1914, the Chicago, Milwaukee and St. Paul Railway and the Oregon-Washington Railroad and Navigation Company joined forces to build the depot known as the Union Depot. The Oregon-Washington Railroad and Navigation Company was owned by Union Pacific. The Union Depot was demolished for room to build the 1974 World Fair. (Courtesy of NRSPL.)

The Washington Water Power depot was built in 1909 and located on Wall Street north of Trent Avenue. They were in competition over streetcar lines in Spokane for years with the Spokane Traction Company. Eventually all the lines merged with Washington Water Power, even the Spokane Traction Company line. The new name of the electric trolley and streetcar system became the Spokane United Railways in 1922. In the 1930s, this system of electric streetcars gave way to automobiles, jitneys, and then motorbuses. (Courtesy of the Gene Hawk Collection.)

The Interurban Passenger Terminal, designed by Albert Held in 1906, was located on Main and Lincoln, where the Spokane Library now stands. Held moved to Spokane Falls right after the fire of 1889, a very advantageous time for a man of his talent. The terminal was built on a large ravine filled with fire debris from the Great Fire of 1889. The terminal was used for the Spokane and Inland Empire Railway and the Spokane Traction Company. (Courtesy of JQCPBCL.)

This picture is of the Union Pacific Railroad locomotive No. 3219, embellished with flags and bunting, stopped at the West Spokane roundhouse in 1923. This locomotive had the honor of pulling 29th president Warren G. Harding's special train. The visit occurred on his way to Alaska, where he created the Naval Petroleum Reserve on November 4, 1923. (Courtesy of Gene Hawk, photograph by H. M. Cowling, from Dick Paul's collection.)

This is a 1915 photograph of the Great Northern Railway yard at Hillyard. This view, from the roof of a steam locomotive erecting shop, faces south toward the Queen Avenue crossing. Hillyard was platted in 1892 and named in honor of James Hill, the Empire Builder of the Great Northern Railway. It was finally annexed into Spokane by 1924. (Courtesy of the Inland Empire Railway Historical Society, Dennison Photo, from Arnie Hovind.)

The Spokane and Inland Railway electric locomotive No. B1 was built to use AC or DC, depending on its location. It was used for light freight hauling and switching. It produced 1200 horsepower and could haul up to 900,000 pounds on a 2-percent grade going at least 8 miles per hour. It was started by Jay Graves to service the Spokane to Palouse areas. (Courtesy of JQCPBCL.)

Francis Cook started the first steam motor trolley in November 16, 1888. His Spokane and Montrose Motor Railroad was powered by steam. It opened transportation from downtown to the Grand and Manito Avenues. In 1902, Jay Graves bought Cook's trolley, which had already been converted into electric, for his son Clyde, and renamed it the Spokane Traction Company. The new competition caused Washington Water and Power to expand their lines to new housing development, which was good for the city. (Courtesy of JQCPBCL.)

One of the worst train disasters in U.S. history occurred on March 1, 1910. Two Seattle-bound Great Northern trains were awaiting passage in one of the worst snowstorms of the century. The Great Northern train No. 25 and a mail train No. 27, owned by James Hill, had been waiting in Wellington since February 23, 1910, due to the snow on the tracks. Supt. James H. O'Neill, shown below, had crews of men working to clear out the snow around the clock. In the morning of the horrible event, a lightning storm struck the snow above the train, creating an avalanche. Ninety-six people died, including: R. M. Barnhart, Charles S. Eltinge, Catherine O'Reilly and Nellie Sharp, all from Spokane. Two of the few survivors were Lewis C. Jesseph and John Merritt, attorneys from Spokane, who hiked out the Sunday before. (Courtesy of JQCPBCL.)

It was not just the railroads that had accidents. On December 18, 1915, the Division Street Bridge collapsed as two streetcars were crossing. Five people were killed and 12 were injured. The electric streetcars belonged to Washington Water Power, with one going southbound and one traveling northbound. The wooden-truss bridge was built in 1888. (Courtesy of Ted Halloway, from JQCPBCL.)

The Palace clothing store in 1925 delivered to homes in Spokane. Their advertisement in the February 4, 1913, *Chronicle* announced that their store, located at Main and Post Street, was a popular cash store for all people. They sold wallpaper rolls for 3¢ each, chocolates, coats for $7.50, and women's patent leather shoes for $1.48. They were known for great service and giving out S&H Green Stamps with every purchase. (Courtesy of JQCPBCL.)

Florence Hafer and her daughter Charlene are sitting in their Buick, built around 1917. They were on a camping trip, with the supplies in the large box strapped to the side and folding chairs along the running board. Virginia Adsit claimed, "My grandmother (Florence) was one of the first women in Spokane to have her own car." Virginia Adsit also remembers her paternal grandmother boiling water in a tea kettle for use in the radiator of her car. Below is Charlene Hafer in her toy car, acting like her mother and practicing her driving. (Courtesy of Virginia Adsit.)

Pine Creek Dairy was built in 1908 on Division St. It was known as the largest dairy in the area and owned by William C. Sohns. They delivered milk, ice cream, cheese, and butter to the people of Spokane. The local children were always excited about seeing the Pine Creek Dairy truck, in the hopes to get their hands on some ice cream. (Courtesy of JQCPBCL.)

This biplane picture is of "A. D. Smith's airplane taking off from Glover Field circa 1912," according to Tony and Suzanne Bamonte in Spokane and the Inland Northwest. This landing happened just a few years after aviation began with the Wright brothers in Kitty Hawk, North Carolina in 1903. Glover Field was used several times in early aviation, but the city fathers soon passed legislation to stop the practice of landing on Glover Field. (Courtesy of Gene Hawk.)

Felts Field is famous for hosting the *Spokane Sun-God*, which was the first airplane piloted by Nicholas Mamer, to make a nonstop transcontinental round-trip, while refueling in flight. Felts Field was established in 1913. In the 1920s, Felts Field became part of the national airmail service. The commercial aircraft moved to Geiger Field during World War II, but private aircraft still used Felts Field. (Courtesy of JQCPBCL.)

The first airplane flight in Spokane was April 2, 1910, by aviator Charles Keeney Hamilton. The *Spokesman-Review* said his final day at the Spokane fair attracted an estimated crowd of 20,000. Hamilton, a successful businessman from Spokane, gave up a large contract with Glenn Curtis of aviation fame, to fly in his hometown. He ended up dying at the young age of 29 from complications of earlier crashes. (Courtesy of the Arthur Peterson Collection, NRSPL.)

Eight

OLMSTED'S GIFT

Francis Cook originally owned Montrose Park, later renamed Manito Park (Manito is the Nez Perce word for "high ground"). The land was later given to the city of Spokane. Charles E. Balzer, the first Manito superintendent, built this arch "See Spokane Shine." Manito had a dance pavilion on Mirror Lake, bands playing, a zoo, Owl Castel (aviary), topiaries in the shape of animals, a playground, Rose, Lilac, Perennial, Sunken and Japanese Gardens. (Courtesy of NRSPL.)

Aubrey L. White, known as the father of Spokane's park system, was president of the Park Board and a garden columnist for the *Spokesman-Review*. He had the brilliant idea of having John Charles Olmsted (stepson of Fredrick Olmsted, of the New York's Central Park fame) complete a park report in 1908. Spokane is still using the Olmsted report for guidance, as they have reclaimed the Riverfront area, Riverside State Park and preserved the natural beauty of the river. John Charles Olmsted and his associate, James Frederick Dawson, laid out these principles to have parks in every neighborhood, yielding many areas for escape and tranquility by keeping parks natural and undeveloped. Duncan Gardens, shown below, was named after John Duncan, the superintendent of Manito for over 32 years. (Above, courtesy of NRSPL; below, courtesy of MAC Naughton Collection, NRSPL.)

416. Sunken!Gardens. Manito Park, Spokane, Wash.

The Bear Pit was a very popular attraction at Manito Park Zoo. They had pairs of polar, grizzly and black bears. The other attractions included, but were not limited to: beavers, elk, a billy goat, four buffalo, an ostrich, emu, cougars, birds, ducks, and coyotes. The zoo finally closed in 1932 due to the city's inability to cover the $3,000 annual operating cost. (Courtesy of NRSPL.)

The little girl sitting on the front steps of the Hafer house is Elizabeth Harris, childhood friend of Charlotte Hafer. On July 10, 1923, nine-year-old Elizabeth was feeding the bears at the Manito Zoo, when a polar bear took off her right arm. It was a sad day that Spokane residents never forgot. The zoo was in existence from 1900 until 1932, finally closing because of hard economic times. (Courtesy of Virginia Adsit.)

Natatorium Park was established in 1889 as the terminus to the WWP Streetcar lines. The area was a development called the Twickenham Park. The park had a baseball diamond, hotel, and casino. After the covered swimming pool was built, the name changed to Natatorium (a separate building containing a swimming pool). One of the most famous attractions was the Looff Carrousel, built in 1909, which was relocated to Riverfront Park after the closure of Natatorium Park in 1960. During its tenure, Natatorium Park was a year-round amusement park. Dorothea Landt remembers sailors from Farragut Naval Training Station enjoying the rides during World War II. The Scenic Railway ride in the 1915 photograph below was one of the amusements. Above, the Shoot the Chutes ride was added in 1907. Riders boarded a flat-bottomed boat and were pulled up a 300-foot-long, 100-foot-high ramp to a tower at the top, then launched down into the water. Many famous people visited the park, such as celebrity Babe Ruth. (Courtesy of Edwin H. Kittilson, Denise Masiello and Gary Nance.)

Charles F. Hafer, manager of the Armour Meat packing company, and his wife, Florence, are enjoying the view of Spokane on top of the rock formation Cliff Park. One of Spokane's oldest parks started from land given to the city by the Northern Pacific Railroad in the 1880s. Kirtland K. Cutter was one of the architects of the Cliff Park District. The image below shows the panoramic view of the city as it is located in the center of Grove Street, Twelfth Avenue, Thirteenth Avenue, and Stevens Street. The trees block some of the view today, but when Cliff Park was first developed, one could see the Manito Park area and far to the north as in the picture below. (Courtesy of Virginia Adsit.)

Del King came from a boxing family with two cousins (Glen and Eddie) in Clayton and Deer Park. Del had a promising future with a powerful left/right combination. He started boxing at the age of 17 and at the time of his death two years later, his record was 28-3-2. Del's girlfriend, Elaine Haynes (pictured kissing), and his sister Lorraine were devastated upon his death. Lorraine was a local professional singer during the later days of the roaring 20s and vaudeville. On March 31, 1921, World Heavyweight Champion boxer Jack Dempsey came to Spokane for a promotion at Allen Racetrack, seen below. "The Manassa Mauler" fought from 1913 until 1927 and was the world champion from 1919 until his loss to Gene Tunney in 1926. (Above, courtesy of DPC; below, courtesy of JQCPBCL.)

Glover Field was built in honor of James Glover in Peaceful Valley, alongside the Spokane River and below the spectacular falls. The approach to Glover Field was from Main Street and the new stadium was built at the east end of Peaceful Valley. It offered open seating at both ends of the field, and was used for football and baseball games, track meets, fairs, and many other events. The stadium was later used as a training camp for semiprofessional boxers. Del King, in the photograph at right, a prominent fighter in the boxing ring, trained at this site. He appeared on cards at Dishman, Spokane, and Seattle. In the background, the Monroe Street Bridge and the Great Northern Railway span the Spokane River. Del died at the age of 19 of septicemia, an infection under his right arm. (Courtesy of DPC.)

Melvin Hein was born in 1909 and was destined to become one of pro football's greatest centers. Playing with the New York Giants from 1931 to 1945, Mel was an All-Pro eight times, league MVP in 1938, and two-time NFL champion. Mel played college football at Washington State University, and in 1930, during his senior year, he was an All-American. In the 1931 Rose Bowl, Mel's team beat Alabama 24-0! Mel was honored in 1930, shown here at the train depot with Miss Spokane Marguerite Motie. Spokane City League baseball began in 1908 and was a "fast" league. Amateur, town teams, and semiprofessional city leagues sprang up all over the Northwest. A local business team was sponsored by the owner of the local B&K grocery, stands in the center of back row of the 1925 photograph. Kneeling on the far left is star slugger Addison "Crusher" Haynes. (Above, courtesy of JQCPBCL; below, courtesy of DPC.)

The Spokane City League, semiprofessional baseball, flourished throughout the Inland Empire and was at its peak in the 1920s and 1930s. The photograph above features a local Spokane team, name unknown, with its manager lying down to the left, and its star first baseman, George Dittmar, in the second row to the far right. George had excellent range and could "hit 'em where they ain't." George prided himself in playing Ty Cobb style baseball, as "rough and ready" was his motto. College baseball was growing in popularity, and Aage Anderson's father was one of the stars of his Spokane College team. Spokane College was located at Twenty-ninth Avenue, just east of Grand Boulevard, and opened it's doors in 1909. Aage was of Norwegian descent and came to America with his family in 1900s. The photograph is dated 1928. (Above, courtesy of DPC; below, courtesy of Aage Anderson.)

Visit us at
arcadiapublishing.com